PRAISE FOR

BRILLIANT DISGUISE

"A double helix of a memoir that intertwines a life in the rock 'n' roll hothouse of late 70s New York with a deeply personal account of a tragic sibling, *Brilliant Disguise* is a moving portrait of innocence and experience."

—Joe Hagan, author of *Sticky Fingers: The Life & Times of Jann Wenner and Rolling Stone Magazine*

"*Brilliant Disguise* recounts Susan's efforts to navigate two male-dominated cultures of the late 1970s—*Rolling Stone* magazine and music promotion. At the same time, her lucid, relatable account probes the formidable private challenges of family crisis, romance, career, and single motherhood. The No Nukes concerts Kellam organized at Madison Square Garden stand out, but so does the plangent elegy for her troubled brother and her stubborn urge to carry on. Although the title quotes a classic Springsteen lyric, let there be no doubt: Susan Kellam is the real thing."

> —Peter Richardson, author of *Savage Journey: Hunter S. Thompson and the Weird Road to Gonzo*

"More than a rock 'n' roll memoir, *Brilliant Disguise* is a heartfelt family saga, written with wit, verve, and compassion by the woman who lived it."

> —Jayne Loader, codirector of the cult classic film, *The Atomic Cafe*

"A book about the bonds of family, which never really loosen. Susan's story will be of great interest to anyone who ever fought the political, sexual, and familial wars."

> —Robert Ward, author of the award-winning novel *Red Baker*

"Brilliant Disguise does what every good memoir should: it shows how our personal journeys help shape the world around us while that world, in turn, helps shape the direction of our lives. The story—set against the fascinating soundscape of New York's rock music scene in the 1970s—is honest and profound."

> —Pam Fessler, former national correspondent for NPR and author of *Carville's Cure: Leprosy, Stigma, and the Fight for Justice.*

"Susan captures the confusion, grunge, and elation of coming of age in New York City in the 1970s while also exploring what led to her brother taking his life. The result is a heady mix of rock 'n' roll, the growth of a political movement, and an understanding of child trauma."

—Charles Light, filmmaker, *Lovejoy's Nuclear War* and *The Last Resort.*

Brilliant Disguise

by Susan Kellam

© Copyright 2024 Susan Kellam

ISBN 979-8-88824-345-9

Published by

◤ köehlerbooks™

3705 Shore Drive
Virginia Beach, VA 23455
800-435-4811
www.koehlerbooks.com

BRILLIANT DISGUISE

a memoir

SUSAN KELLAM

VIRGINIA BEACH
CAPE CHARLES

FOR JUSTIN, JENNA, AND REID—
HIS LEGACY; MY JOY.

I MADE IT ALL UP.
THAT'S HOW GOOD I AM.
—BRUCE SPRINGSTEEN

CHAPTER 1

Two siblings, we were.

When our nuclear family exploded into a vaporous mushroom cloud, Robert and I could only, as Bert the Turtle jingled in civil-defense cartoons, duck and cover. Mom took us to live with Grandma Rose in a rambling house in the Baltimore suburbs that had, in lieu of a bomb shelter, a vast basement stacked with wooden crates from Grandpa Abe's soda bottling business. After Grandpa died, the business went under around the same time that Dad left, his six-foot-two frame bent double, and our lives were indelibly altered.

Robert, at six, watched from his bedroom window as Dad left that day from our packed-up home. Three years younger, I had been given a weathergirl kit with vinyl rain gear to distract me from the yelling. My small fingers were kept busy as I tugged the umbrella from its sheath and heard everything being said.

"I didn't do this to destroy you, Annette." Then Dad's voice lowered. "I made a mistake."

A yell. "Your mistake cost us everything."

A plea. "I can make things all right again for us."

"There is no *us*. I can't trust you anymore."

"I don't want to leave the kids."

"You should have considered them before you made a mess of our lives."

Loud ricocheting words that hurt my ears, then vocal cracking and sobs, followed by more angry words that I did not understand. I heard the door shut. We would not see our father again for nearly a year.

Much confusion surrounded our sudden transition from a square brick house in Sudbrook Park to our grandmother's house in Pikesville. Mom disappeared many mornings to a large closed room downtown. "Stifling in there," would be all she said upon returning in the evenings too tired to give us hugs. How desperately we needed affection, or at least some sign that our drastically changed lives would not continue to disintegrate until no one and nothing remained.

We stopped asking about Dad.

Then his crimes blared into headline news. *The Baltimore Morning Sun,* August 28, 1957: "LAWYERS ACT ON KELLAM . . . Disbarment or disciplinary action was sought before the Supreme Bench yesterday against Sidney I. Kellam, Baltimore attorney, on the grounds that he has been guilty of 'fraudulent and highly improper conduct unbecoming and unworthy of a member of the bar.'" *The Baltimore Evening Sun*, October 4, 1957: "LAWYER FACES 3 CHARGES . . . Three criminal charges today were entered by the Baltimore grand jury against Sidney I. Kellam . . ." *The Baltimore Morning Sun,* December 20, 1957: "LAWYER GUILTY IN EMBEZZLING. Sidney I. Kellam, 34-year-old Baltimore attorney, yesterday was convicted of embezzling funds . . . Judge John T. Tucker suspended a one-year prison sentence on condition Kellam make restitution . . . Judge Tucker was told the lawyer will not contest disbarment." *The Baltimore Evening Sun,* December 20, 1957: "LAWYER RECEIVES SUSPENDED SENTENCE."

In the chaos that ensued, the adults brushed us aside. Yet Robert and I heard everything, especially Mom's sisters telling her what a monster Dad was and that she should never even consider forgiving him. She should push for a divorce immediately. The best thing our father could do for his family, they said, would be to take his life. I escaped this vicious barrage of words by tunneling through imaginary worlds. But Robert could read and would have filtered those multiple-syllable charges against our father through a highly vulnerable young mind. There was no thought in the 1950s of how children might react to this dramatic turn of events. One day our father was a major part of our lives; then, in a flash, he was gone. Worse, he was being vilified. If he was so horrid, what were we, his children? Mom was unable to provide us with any way to understand these strange events or to offer emotional support. We had no ability to fill the gap in our hearts. We could only act out.

One day Robert dug a hole in the lawn, somewhere between the driveway and the front door. In the dark, my mother tripped and sprained her ankle. Seemingly innocent child's play, no one considered it might have something to do with sudden and unexplained loss.

I once followed the TV repair man into the den where Mom slept at night on the green sofa and asked, "Do you have a little girl?"

He put down his toolbox. "Yes, I do."

"Does she live with you?"

"Let the nice man fix the television now, Susie." Carrie, the tiny gray-haired African-American woman who cleaned my grandmother's house and kept an eye on us, managed to coax me into another room.

I was somehow able to fill my tiny world with sunlight streaming through crystal prisms that dangled from the dining room chandelier, casting rainbows for me to chase. Or, I would run to the living room, where a grand piano gave me shelter to converse with a bevy of imaginary friends. If Grandma Rose was home, I could go into her bedroom and curl beside her as she watched *Dialing for Dollars, Queen for a Day*, and other endless game shows. We never talked; just lay there and watched to see who would win.

Robert and I shared the other bedroom, the most-special room in the house because we were together and I wasn't alone when bitter words from Mom and Grandma penetrated our closed door, the edge of their voices sharpened by missed child support checks and a frustration that made no sense to me. They were grownups and could do anything they pleased. I was powerless. Even Robert could cross Stevenson Road, pedal to the "lot"—an undeveloped acre in the neighborhood where the boys gathered to throw balls—and stay up past nine o'clock watching *Twilight Zone* while I lay in bed trying to add up the days until I received such a windfall.

It wasn't that my world was so bad in the large house Grandpa Abe had designed for his later years, years that never came. Mom cooked us fudge every Friday night and, in winter, we made popcorn in the fireplace. My cousins lived right up the hill and we often played together. Their dad—Uncle Morty, who had married Mom's youngest sister, Shifra—was the richest man I knew. An auditorium at the synagogue named after his family showcased a big shiny plaque in tribute.

Everyone rich was Jewish in Pikesville, a northwest suburb of Baltimore, a neighborhood of delis and comfortable homes. Every *important* person was Jewish. The one Christian boy in my class had pants too short and a ripped book bag. He took the school bus in from an older neighborhood where houses were small, the grass brown, and old tires lay on the front yards.

I poked Robert one day. "John Kennedy is Jewish."

"What makes you think our president is Jewish?" He taunted me, as he did when he wanted to squash me down to worm size.

"Because he's rich and important," I answered.

"John Kennedy is Catholic. He's the first Catholic president ever."

Robert leaned over to where I was tossing a handful of metal jacks. "Ever."

I bounced the ball and scooped only two jacks before catching it. Just when I thought I had figured out the way the world worked, Robert went and flattened it. Some things were better kept tightly locked away from Robert the bulldozer.

"Lyndon Johnson isn't Jewish either," Robert continued. "He's Texan."

I didn't want to hear any more, so I started to hum, shutting my eyes to get a better picture. The darkness had its own color, sometimes whirling colors. Robert penetrated my kaleidoscope, saying, "Face it Susan, we're a minority. Grandma, Mom, you, and me."

My eyes flashed open. "What about Dad?"

"What about him?"

Though we hadn't seen him, he was *still* our dad. Mom and Grandma Rose bickered constantly about all the money he owed. I would learn that the large closed room where Mom had disappeared for days was a courtroom where many lawyers argued over my father's fate. Only a bundle of cash, for restitution and exorbitant legal fees, kept him out of jail. Most of that bundle had come from Grandpa Abe, before he died, before the lucrative soda-bottling business he ran collapsed and money became such a pressing problem.

◆　◆　◆

We were five and eight when Dad returned. He took us to Gwynn Oak Amusement Park, loud with screams emanating from its Big and Little Dippers and Wild Mouse. Groups of protestors often picketed the segregated park in the fifties and sixties. All I saw was the other car that pulled over shortly after we had parked, and my father looking adoringly at someone getting out. I was struck by the woman's red hair and how quickly she joined us.

"Kids," Dad said. "Meet Shirley."

I stared until Robert pinched me. "Say hello to the lady," he whispered.

"Are we still going on the rides?" I asked instead.

The pretty woman knelt down and cupped my hands inside the softness of her leather gloves. "What ride do you want to go on first?" she asked.

"What one that Robbie does." Robert was still Robbie then.

"Let's go," Dad said, as he swept me up in his arms. "We'll ride them all."

Dad and Shirley were already married that day at Gwynn Oak. We just didn't know. Our father juggled multiple jobs and speculated for land deals while Shirley worked as a secretary to keep food on the table. They also managed a motel, a rent-free place to live.

When Dad picked us up for our first weekend at the Vagabond Motel in Aberdeen, Maryland, I waited for many long minutes at the end of the asphalt driveway, swinging my tiny suitcase. Robert was hiding in the basement when Dad drove up.

"Nice place, Dad," Robert said when we finally got there. I knew he didn't mean that.

Getting out of the car, getting a ground perspective, I imagined that each separate motel room opened into a bright, colorful world. Behind us was Route 40, lines of cars whizzing past at fifty miles an hour, making so much noise I could hardly think. Dad said the cars were going to New York City. I wanted to see the inside of a motel room and escape the street sounds. But rather than opening one of those doors, Dad led us around to the back to an old house.

"I want to stay in a motel room," I whined.

"Can you pay for it?" Dad shot back.

I followed him up wooden rickety steps, no longer swinging my suitcase. Later, as it grew dark, Shirley took us on her evening rounds. We trailed out of the big house and rounded the corner to the front, where the Vagabond stretched out its two limbs and embraced Route 40, ablaze in headlights. She showed us the small gaslights by each room covered with cut-glass lids that fell snugly into metal rims, then lifted me up to pull off the first glass cover. Robert got to hold out the spark gun that ignited the gas into a golden flame. There were fifteen to light, one next to each closed-tight door.

Robert held that spark gun like a soldier on a long march.

Lights glimmered inside several of the rooms, and I became more convinced than ever that these rooms, licked a golden brown by gas flames, contained secrets. There was magic here. There had to be. It was my dad's place.

Only later, in bed, did I admit to my brother that I was a little scared at the Vagabond, this big old place with so many doors and rooms and odd people coming and going; guys in Army uniforms and fancy ladies who called me sweetie, buzzing the bells, asking for a bed; noises from the highway of gravel shooting and rubber skidding.

Robert stayed quiet. Yet I could hear his wide-awake breathing, so different from when he slept. He asked, "You all right, Susie?"

I let out a plaintive "Noooo."

"Want to get in bed with me?"

Without answering, I slipped out from under my covers and hopped barefoot to the other bed. We lay together for a few minutes in silence. Then the scratching began, like an army of elephants on rodent feet marching through the walls. We formed a tent with our upright knees, a fortress against any invasion. Robert reached out and pulled in a flat round metal ashtray. "It's a flying saucer," he said to me. "It can take us anywhere we want to go."

Even in our dark tent, I could see Robert's huge dark eyes glowing in the charcoal air. "If you had your brother's eyes," my mother once said, "you'd be so pretty."

The shiny ashtray Robert held between us picked up the dusty light in our tent and reflected it back. "You decide," he said.

"Can we go back in time?"

"Sure. But don't say anything. Stay very quiet. Just think about where you want to be. Think really hard."

I tried to imagine when Dad lived with us in Sudbrook Park and took a bus downtown every day to his law office in the city of Baltimore. Before I could picture him in a suit, I drifted into sleep, cuddled close to my brother. Safety.

◆　◆　◆

By high school, in the midsixties, Robert was every girl's heartthrob, his eyes a deep brown velvet, his youthful form a wrestler's tight physique. Though only five foot eight, everyone called him "Big K." I trailed after as "Little K."

Robert was the one most likely to succeed.

I was the one most likely to do foolish things, fall in love with the wrong men, and leap headlong after college into New York City without a job or a place to stay. Events converged and converged again. Never musically inclined, I nonetheless got hired by *Rolling Stone* magazine when they staffed up in preparation for the big move from San Francisco to glitzy offices overlooking Central Park. I gravitated toward the more political work being done at the magazine and eventually became part of five nights of benefit concerts at Madison Square Garden to raise money for No Nukes. Determined to live life fully, I inevitably got snared in the rock politics scramble and, bruised, escaped to our father's house; by then, Dad lived in central Pennsylvania, having deftly patched up his life by converting farmlands into shopping centers and industrial parks.

Addled by lack of sleep and drug-induced paranoia, one day I took refuge by a fast-running creek at the edge of the property, staring at the sky and the tops of trees with leaves just barely tinged by autumn's nearness. Believing myself right on the brink of going stark raving mad, I looked toward the horizon, as far as I could see. Going crazy would put me over that edge, into the beyond. I stared at the distant line that nature had softened with filtered light and wavering treetops. I could cross that line, cross over that horizon.

Would that be so terrible?

I lay there for a long time, waiting for the horizon to move in, encroach, and beckon me over. Prepared to disappear into deep oblivion, I was ready.

"Susan."

A familiar voice and the rustling of leaves.

"Susan."

My brother's face replaced the endless horizon, giving me arms to hold, keeping me from falling off the earth's edge.

"I figured I'd find you here."

I sat up, lightheaded but with a rush of relief. I was safe.

Such sibling love and protection would always be there, I wrongly assumed.

◆   ◆   ◆

In the early morning of June 4, 1990, Robert kissed his wife and two sleeping children goodbye and drove off. He did not head directly to work; instead, he kept driving all day and into the night. We don't know, will never know, where he went or what jagged thoughts ripped through his mind. A worker in Robert's shirt-manufacturing factory found him the next morning. Hanging.

I was at a Capitol Hill bar in Washington that evening with two Associated Press reporters—my boyfriend, Dick Keil, in the throes of covering Washington Mayor Marion Barry's drug and prostitution trial, and John King, the wire service's top political reporter. They dared me to drink a shot of tequila, and then another.

Hungover the next morning, I was blurringly stunned when a cousin showed up at my Virginia workplace to drive me the sixty miles to Baltimore. Jill didn't want to tell me what happened. But I knew.

My answering machine, when I checked it that morning after returning home from Dick's apartment, had beeped out two hang ups. Had Robert been trying to reach me? And during the night, when I'd gone to the bathroom, a distinctive whish of cool air had rubbed past. Was he saying goodbye?

Many questions and scattered clues remain strewn throughout Robert's thirty-nine years. Recalling the events is not an exact replay of the past as it happened. According to Charan Ranganath, author of the 2024 book *Why We Remember: Unlocking Memory's Power to Hold on to What Matters,* we look at our memories through a lens of interpretation and imagination. In doing so, Ranganath suggests, we can sometimes gain wisdom.

I consider this memoir exactly that: my effort to extract meaning and wisdom from what is written in my many journals and from those images that have stayed with me. Understanding my brother's last desperate act has required going back to difficult moments, combing through nearly forgotten exchanges for some retrospective meaning, and teasing out what I missed.

And, why I survived.

CHAPTER 2

How to describe a brother who for years loomed as the center of my universe. The young me basked in his glow. Teachers singled me out because, certainly, the little sister would excel too. But how could I ever reach their expectations? Girls befriended me to get invited over, see where he slept, what posters hung in his room. Three varsity letters and a state wrestling championship.

Also, the intangibles, what cannot easily be put into words. Call it charisma, three rhythmic syllables that could never hit the same perfect pitch as Robert in his day-to-day interactions. He knew how to listen, taking everything in with warm, soothing eyes. Those with less popularity would never be shoved aside on Friday nights when the cool kids gathered in the parking lot behind the Suburban House deli. My brother embraced people, clasped each and every one like vital beings, made them feel special. Even I, two grades behind, somehow slipped through and ran with the in-crowd. Otherwise, I would have been home curled up with a book. Shy, flat-chested, stringy-haired, no one would have noticed me, except, I was Little K.

We had moved during the elementary-school years to a small apartment in a new complex by the railroad tracks that, though barely more than a partitioned rectangle, provided Robert with his own room and a door that locked. I shared the room across the hall with Mom; Grandma Rose had the third bedroom. There was no place for me to hide or to bring friends. That didn't matter for Robert, as his cavalcade of pals and girlfriends would have followed him anywhere.

Such a large presence as my brother could sometimes become overly protective. Robert tried to shield me as I slowly bloomed, found verve, rebelled. I met Billy the summer after my junior year of high school at an antiwar protest on the Johns Hopkins campus. He took me back to where he lived with two other students and lit a marijuana joint. I had never been stoned, but lied when I grabbed the roach clip and took a large hit. I lied again when Billy asked if I was a virgin, giving him a sly smile from under the dark lines I had drawn around my eyes with a cheap eyeliner pencil. It was easy to peel off my skin-tight white shorts that night and follow him to bed. He penetrated me quickly and, though it hurt, I managed to stifle any sounds.

Later, Billy asked me what I wanted to do with my life. I would be leaving for college in less than a year.

"Get out of Baltimore."

He laughed. "People always come home."

"I won't."

"You'll get married."

"No, I won't."

"What then?"

How could I explain that I'd been wrapped inside myself for sixteen years? Coiled like a snail, I just wanted to crack that shell and escape.

Robert stood outside our garden apartment building when Billy drove me home. Not a hostile presence but a rebuke. He shook Billy's hand with a firm grip. A warning, far too late. Inside, I undressed quietly, slipped into my single bed in the shared room. I did not wake up Mom. A part of me had already moved on.

Our mother had worked for Baltimore City, checking on welfare moms to make sure no man lived with them and that the kids were safe. She had done similar work before marriage had taken her to Charlottesville, where Dad earned his law degree on the GI Bill at the University of Virginia. Mom resumed social work after the divorce. Being a caseworker gave my mother a cadre of colleagues of her intellectual equal. The job also grounded her perspective on being at the bottom. We had it good, she assured us. We did not live in the high-rise public housing that bred crime in downtown Baltimore. Eventually, after the city required case workers to have a master's degree, she tried teaching inner-city high school students. She would come home miserable, moan about the kids' rude behavior, and fix a large Bloody Mary. Had it gone on any longer, I might have worried about my mother's sobriety. She eventually found a less-demanding job as social director at a nearby apartment complex.

We mostly lived off Grandma Rose's social security check. When the old car broke down, that check bought us a new one, a sparkling white Chevrolet convertible, used but presentable. Soon enough the collapsible roof sprung leaks, and the floor gave way in the back. The Floorless Flyer, Robert proudly declared.

◆   ◆   ◆

Robert started college in 1969 at Pennsylvania State University. What a brouhaha that caused. With good test scores, high grades, varsity letters, and strong recommendations, he had gotten into every college where he applied. Mom wanted him to go to the University of Virginia. Dad, who had recently moved to Harrisburg, bribed Robert with a car if he chose Penn State.

When my brother left for college, I took over his bedroom, careful not to rearrange anything or replace record albums in the wrong slots. Even the framed copy of the Gettysburg Address on parchment that Mom had hung, and Robert left behind, would remain untouched.

One weekend I joined his girlfriend Faye, a beautiful Greek-American with green eyes flecked with black, on a bus trip to State College in the height of autumn on winding highways through forests of changing hues. Her parents refused to let her go unless I went. Though just a cover, that did not bother me. I couldn't wait to see a college campus and my brother. Immediately upon arrival, Robert drove us to a fraternity house.

"There is where you'll stay," he told me.

"What about you and Faye?" I looked at them. Both gorgeously dark and vivid, like entwined mirror images.

Robert looked away when he rhetorically asked, "What about us?"

I had been so excited to visit my brother at college; instead, I was to fend for myself. Only a junior in high school, being abandoned in a college frat house had the mark of true adventure stirred with a delicious dash of risk. But I knew my brother would not have brought me there if real danger lurked.

Robert led me up dimly lit circular steps and into someone's room. A pungent smoky odor filled my nose. "This is where Damien lives. If he likes you, you'll get a spot on the bed. Otherwise, you may have to sleep on the floor."

That was the last I saw of Robert and Faye that weekend until shortly before our return bus departed. Penn State presented a weekend of many firsts for me: Hanging with Damien as he tripped on LSD, listening to Elton John sing "Your Song" through headphones at a record store in the middle of the night, and being given an entire bottle of wine to drink.

I would gladly have returned to Penn State, but Robert flunked out his first year. He had used the car Dad gave him to drive back to Baltimore every chance he got to be with Faye and hardly ever went to classes. A crisis ensued, one requiring our father's presence in the apartment to talk directly with Mom. Robert had not yet returned home.

A large looming figure, my dad made our tiny dining area look like a dollhouse miniature. "How could this happen?" he bellowed. He refused to sit down.

I was supposed to disappear, but no spot in that tiny apartment took me out of earshot. Dad rattled off questions. "Why didn't we know he was doing so poorly?" "Did he say anything to you?" "Nothing came in the mail?"

My distraught mother had no answers. They agreed Robert would have to come home, take summer classes, and start at the University of Maryland in the fall. Faye would be at College Park, so perhaps Robert got exactly what he wanted. Except, more likely, this uncharacteristic behavior was beyond his control. Doing so miserably at college after a stellar high school career signaled distress, even in an era marked by student drop-outs and campus-wide strikes against the Vietnam War. Robert wasn't storming campus buildings or joining Washington-bound caravans. He was silently defying everyone's expectations of him. But no conversations occurred to try to determine what might be happening beneath the surface, how a lethal mix of emotions bottled tight within him for more than a decade had begun to stealthily discharge.

I felt horribly sad for him at the pit of my stomach but didn't know what to do except slowly remove my scattered belongings from the bedroom that was never mine. That was the summer he stood guard the night Billy drove me home late, my virgin innocence gone. Robert probably knew by the independent smirk on my face when I strode past him and into the apartment that I was breaking away. He too moved on, picked himself up after the Penn State fiasco, ran with his crowd, Faye by his side, seemingly happy to be back in Baltimore.

Inevitably, our paths diverged.

I chose the University of Wisconsin in Madison because reaching that Midwest city required two plane trips, a cumbersome and costly journey that limited trips home. I found such summer jobs as being a car-hop waitress at an A&W restaurant and filling mugs with tapped beer at the student union. Surrounded by lakes Mendota, Monona, and Wingra, I learned to sail and waterski. I missed Robert, sure, but distance from him gave me the opportunity to finally develop into my offbeat self, and happily so. I could try LSD. I could, with the pressure to measure up to him lifted, become an honors student. Navigating a large world where no one knew of Big K unshackled me to do anything.

After graduating college, followed by backpacking for five months through Europe, I arrived in the Big Apple as the tall ships were sailing away from New York harbor after the 1976 Bicentennial fireworks. It was the year when gonzo-journalist Hunter Thompson's endorsement of Jimmy Carter in *Rolling Stone* magazine won more votes for Carter than it lost. The magazine's editor and publisher, Jann Wenner, threw a tremendous party in New York for the candidate from Georgia. Not long after, Wenner abruptly decided to relocate the San Francisco tabloid to the East Coast entertainment capital. The so-called San Francisco sounds—Grateful Dead, Jefferson Airplane, the Who—had gone national. Hendrix and Joplin were dead. Wenner wanted to be where things were alive and, newly arrived in New York, I wanted to be part of that massive transition.

CHAPTER 3

My new three-piece tweed suit hung on me awkwardly as I reached the building between Madison and Park avenues where *Rolling Stone* magazine had its small New York base in December 1976. I opened the jacket and loosened the blouse under my vest, swiveled the skirt so that the zipper followed the curve of my hip. The bag over my shoulder slid to the crook of my arm as I removed a brush for one last attempt at taming long strands of wind-blown hair before getting on the elevator.

Framed covers of *Rolling Stone* melded into a screaming montage of larger-than-life personalities on the hallway walls: John and Paul, Mick and Keith, Janis and Jimi. Staring at those icons, I felt reverence and awe; in their company, even a tittle of hope.

I asked a woman sitting in an alcove where I might find Iris Brown. Behind which closed door might my interviewer be sitting?

Music blared from some of those offices, and loud combative voices echoed from others.

"Iris isn't in yet."

Lunchtime was drawing close, even in the next time zone.

A few minutes went by before the woman introduced herself. "I'm Lyssa Waters by the way. I assume you're another job applicant for the editorial staff job. We've had quite a parade of people."

My chances of marching far in this parade might have been slim, but I was in the door and feeling confident. I was determined to at least be heard.

Lyssa suggested that I sit down and wait, then returned to her desk, which, like her, had a sense of upheaval. Cluttered papers fell to the floor and, as Lyssa scrambled to pick things up, her thick curly hair loosened from its pins.

Rod Stewart stared at me from the most recent issue of the magazine—one not yet on the newsstand—that included a teaser for a story on the death of Karen Silkwood. I ignored Rod and turned to the dead girl, reading through the details with lurid fascination. I had never heard of Karen Silkwood, this person who had been on her way to meet a *New York Times* reporter with evidence of faulty nuclear reactor fuel rods when her car crashed into a culvert. Even thwarted, the article made her into a martyr.

A bit of the devil in Karen, sassy, everyone who had known her said. Wild for a single working mom of three, she enjoyed her booze and drugs and said anything on her mind. Freely applied mascara made her dark eyes glow in a pale slender face, and few could deny her physical effect on people. Growing more intrigued as I read, I barely noticed how long I had been there. Karen Silkwood, her life and her death, tugged at something in me, a restlessness to cross my own safety line.

I looked at the article's byline: Howard Kohn.

After I had sat reading for an hour or so, Lyssa walked out of her office and told me that Iris would not be in that day, and I should come back tomorrow at the same time. Lyssa and another editorial staffer were tallying the results of a recent reader survey and did not have time to talk. I left with Rod Stewart curled under my arm, still hopeful I would find a job.

◆ ◆ ◆

I had gotten my first glimpse of the city's underground music scene as an unpaid intern at *Seven Days* magazine, founded by activist Dave Dellinger to be a *Time* magazine of the left. One day, one of the writers had brought in a poetry rap sheet from a Patti Smith concert the prior night.

"Who is Patti Smith?" I asked.

They all looked at me as if I had asked who Bob Dylan was.

The writer explained how Patti performed *rapping verse.* "It's a powerful form of communication."

I told them how I had witnessed the power of music while visiting Prague, having befriended two young men who could speak to me in the broken English they had gleaned from listening to the explosion of rock and roll pouring out of London and San Francisco. The lyrics revealed to my Prague friends a culture the Soviets had tried to wall off. "They peppered sentences with Mick Jagger's single-syllables—*let's spend night*—and spouted Joplin Americanisms like *kozmic blues.*"

"But that's so sixties," someone said. "Patti Smith is now."

My musical ignorance had not stopped me from applying to *Rolling Stone* magazine when word spread that Jann Wenner would be packing up and moving his San Francisco operation to Manhattan's Fifth Avenue. *Rolling Stone* had dramatically transformed rock journalism, notching it up to a level that fully embraced the unpredictable culture that had spawned the music. Soaring success during its nearly ten years in print was putting the tabloid into the hands of an ever-widening demographic. Perhaps the pages had not often fallen into my hands, but I knew that *Rolling Stone* epitomized a cool, crazy, entirely novel form of writing. This magazine could make or break new musical talent.

Soon after I got the call to come in for an interview, I had gone to Harrisburg to pick up what I'd stored in my father's basement. Before driving me back to the city, Dad took me to one of the discount outlets in a mall that he had built and let me pick out the three-piece blue-and-gray tweed suit I wore for my first interview attempt.

"You eating okay?" Dad asked in the large Buick that he drove on cruise control up the Jersey Turnpike. His dog Andy, a large standard poodle with gray corkscrews, dangled over his shoulder from the backseat, drooling. He and the dog were inseparable.

"Do I look thin?"

"You can gain weight on rice and beans same as steak."

"I eat fine."

"Have you talked to your brother?"

I had sent Robert postcards, from Ireland, Switzerland, and many other countries. My missives breezy: . . . *Traveling is exciting—we've been moving quickly—camping out, hosteling and bed & breakfast, hitching, trains, buses and boats. All My Love, Susan.*

Distance had crept between us but did not deter my thoughts always running toward him, my forever-shining brother encircled by his coterie of friends.

"I called him the other day. He sounds good." Robert always sounded upbeat. "He wished me luck on my job interview."

Dad quickly interjected, "Don't accept lower than what you think you're worth when they start talking salary."

"No one has offered me a job."

"Tell them up front what you're worth."

"I will," I lied.

"Don't shit a shitter."

When we arrived outside my apartment building on the Upper East Side, Dad pushed a wad of cash into my hand, said, "I did well last weekend in Atlantic City." He would always be a gambler.

◆ ◆ ◆

I returned to *Rolling Stone* the second time with a much stronger gait. Since I could not return in the same suit, I found among the clothes retrieved from Harrisburg a slimmer-cut felted skirt and a brightly colored sweater that covered the missing buttons on the skirt waistband. I used a faux silk scarf as a headband to guard my face from flying hair.

Iris Brown was already there when I walked through the door the second time. No taller than me, skinny and dark, something about her—a blend of fragility and brittle strength, a smile that transformed her pertness into exotic beauty, talking with hands that would never drop or lose anything—instantly drew me in. More than that, especially when she laughed, no one could turn away from her magnetism.

That was what I saw. We connected like kindred spirits that day, two Jewish girls from broken homes who wanted far more from life than to keep kosher for a mensch with money. She had become Jann Wenner's chief assistant by peeling out of her ghetto life in the Bronx just as I had escaped the Jewish suburbs of Baltimore.

"Can you type?" Iris shifted quickly between intimacy and interviewer.

"Thirty words per minute."

"Errors?"

"None." Lucky for me, no typing test followed.

She wanted to know more: what had brought me to New York, to apply for *Rolling Stone*?

I began my story. She cut me off.

"Do you like music?"

"Yes, of course."

"What do you listen to?"

"Paul McCartney and Wings. Dylan. Patti Smith." I stopped. "Oh, and Rod Stewart."

"Have you listened to the Ramones or Kiss?"

Though I did not know who they were, I nodded.

She disappeared for a moment. I could hear her sneakers slapping toward the next office, and whispering. I didn't breathe until she returned. She was taking me to meet a senior editor, Paul Scanlon.

Paul sat behind his desk with my resume laid out like a silent prayer. He flicked a lit cigarette into his ashtray and then slipped it back between his lips. How old he seemed with worry lines on his thin handsome face and gray stripes in his dark wavy hair, though he was barely thirty. Legend had it he had been the one to spot the raw insane gonzo talent that became Dr. Hunter S. Thompson. Many more *Rolling Stone* writers owed their early opportunity to Paul. That Paul listened to jazz and was crazy for movies worked in my favor.

He stared at the top of my resume: Assistant for the Second New York International Festival of Women's Films.

"Tell me about this."

The daring female festival organizers, who sought to counter the male-dominated New York Film Festival that runs every fall at Lincoln Center, had needed someone willing to sit in the office rather than run off to view all the films and festivities. Volunteers flocked to the festival, but none wanted desk-job responsibilities. Except for me. I was also the only one who got paid.

I only told him, "It was a great opportunity to see films and meet the filmmakers."

"What was your favorite?"

"Jeanne Moreau's *Lumière*. I like how the storyline shifts between four women's lives."

Paul and I talked for a solid hour with no mention of rock and roll. I told him about the research I was doing on communist films. A new friend I met at the women's film festival was researching and ghostwriting pioneer film distributor Tom Brandon's book on social and political films of the 1930s. As I was cheap labor, Jayne Loader hired me to go to the New York University library in the hours I wasn't job-hunting to photocopy articles from the *Daily Worker.* Streaming through the Communist Party newspaper on microfilm, I couldn't help reading articles by Richard Wright, Woody Guthrie, and others. I learned the meaning of the word *dissident*, a word I could mentally sound out and feel just a bit braver.

Paul offered me a cigarette and I accepted. Since visiting Paris, I had been rolling my own cigarettes but didn't want to reach into my purse and slow down our conversation. I knew there were other applicants for this editorial staff position. *A parade of people*. And I knew that the longer I could hold Paul Scanlon's attention, the better chance I had of getting the job.

I did not want to return to Baltimore. That girl who had slept every night on a single bed next to her mother could not be resurrected. I had spent four years of college pounding her into someone else. Every time I got on a graffiti-speckled, rumbling New York subway and reached for a strap, I knew I was grabbing on to something taking me in the right direction.

CHAPTER 4

Masses of people came to Robert's funeral. Everyone stunned, devastated, confused. My mother broken. My father overnight an old man. Robert's widow, Charlene, clutching the children. How could someone so golden, so loved, so depended upon, simply leave us? Rabbi Mark Loeb cited scripture in Robert's eulogy to offer clues:

"His spirit of light and luminescence is best described in a meaningful image presented by the Bible when it describes the candelabrum, or menorah, first erected by Moses in the wilderness. It had many shafts of light, says Scripture, but the light in the center was brighter than the others, even though it had the same amount of oil as the others. Why was this the case? Because, of all the lights, it alone was positioned to receive the light of the others and then to reflect it back to them, thus adding the reflective glow of their light as it projected its own. Our sages say that this is the nature of love and of a loving person—one who is both capable of giving his own love and also of returning what others give in added quantities. That, pure and simple, was Robert."

I thought of Robert cracking jokes with me.

I had recently bought a computer and quickly became befuddled by the information required to get the machine up and running. As in any perplexing moment, I called my brother.

"What's it asking you?" Just the sound of his voice would always relax me.

"For a serial number."

"Check the box. It should be on the label."

"Found it."

"What else?"

"My name."

"Easy. What else?"

I input the information and clicked through. "My address."

"No!"

"What?"

"Susan," he proclaimed in a faux-haughty tone, "never ever tell a computer where you live."

That was our last conversation.

The rabbi said it well, how my brother magnified love. Robert had been my only dependable male relationship; his love overshadowed everything, even the truth. Unlike my other relationships, I had expected Robert would be there forever. Unlike those other men, Robert was not replaceable.

Such a dizzying array of men in my life, often types I could never take home to meet family. And one that I did take home but should not have. John had the distinction of being a fired air traffic controller who wound up jailed after the PATCO—Professional Air Traffic Controllers Organization—strike in 1981. By the time I met him in the mideighties, John was working for the AFL-CIO, organizing a PATCO replacement union. As a transportation reporter in Washington, I never expected to be totally redirected by his Irish-blue eyes.

We first met in Chicago at an air traffic controllers' convention in 1986. John was already a source, someone who I called regularly for quotes and background information. We often joked. Like Robert, John had surface wit and deep wisdom. When John walked through the doors of the auditorium that day, wit and wisdom was not what grabbed me. He broke through the crowd to approach me. "You must be Susan." I knew the Jersey twang instantly but had never imagined the distinctive cadence flowing from such a cocky smile and tall, erect body, one that looked exactly right in a well-tailored suit.

We shook hands. For once, I was speechless.

"No questions today?" the man of the hour asked. With the vote approaching on certifying the new union, John was featured in *People* magazine. I had not seen the article, or I would have seen the photo and known. Instead, I was Fanny Brice staring for the first time at Nicky Arnstein.

Many months of intense flirting between us went on before something actually happened: I was sideswiped on I-395 driving from Capitol Hill. I called John to pick me up at the police station, my car roped to a tow truck. That I called him, and not anyone else, signaled my willingness.

Did I know he was married? He never hid that fact, not at any point during the two years we carried out a very open and passionate affair. He proposed marriage over a box of saltwater taffy on the Atlantic City boardwalk and did, in time, leave his wife. We even signed a lease together on a rent-control townhouse in Georgetown. And he moved in.

Robert was furious at me for getting involved with a married man and refused to even discuss it. Our conversations those two years were always brisk; my calls not always returned. When I brought John to Baltimore for a family gathering, Robert refused to attend.

But when John inevitably returned to his wife, Robert never once said that he had warned me.

Many of my friends would lament how I had thrown away two years of my life being entangled with John. The implication being that I could have found someone more appropriate while some faint blush of my youth still lingered. I view the real casualty of that ill-fated relationship as my semiestrangement from Robert. Had I known that time with Robert would be so limited would I have embarked on such a poorly destined relationship? I like to think that I would not have allowed myself to be swayed by this married man. But I did so many foolish things, and so many of them were self-destructive. Robert hated seeing me gambling with my chances for a stable future, and he often tried to steer me onto a stronger course.

I, however, did not know—could not see—how my brother's daily activities were gradually building toward his point of no return. Only in retrospect does some of it become clear.

Although I had not seen John for more than a year when my brother died, I called my ex-lover to let him know. Maybe I was accusatory when we spoke. At that point, I truly despised John for being an obstacle during that precious final time with my brother. When John sent me flowers in condolence, I asked that they be immediately taken away and given to a nursing home.

There are many reasons why flowers are an inappropriate solace for Jewish people in mourning. The one I prefer is that death is considered the end of a phase of life, but not of existence. Life, according to Jewish scripture, is eternal. Flowers, while beautiful, are ephemeral, a brief flash of beauty that fades away. Why represent a loved one's existence with something that will not last?

Another reason is more practical, that Jewish burials are done simply and quickly, without extravagances like floral arrangements. There is something all wrong, though, about the haste of a Jewish burial. We have no time to become acclimated to the loss before we must, somehow, coherently make decisions.

Facing the shock of Robert's death in a tequila haze was surreal.

I had been driven to Baltimore and dropped off, my car still in Virginia and my dog stuck alone inside my Georgetown home. My mother's townhouse was crammed with well-meaning family, friends, and neighbors. I walked into that jabbering entourage without any bearings.

I tried to console my mother who had not slept all night, wondering where her son was, why he hadn't reached out to anyone since early morning, absent from work all day. While I was being double dared by two AP reporters to swill shots of tequila, she had descended into hell. I led her upstairs, managing to escape the people and sit alone with her.

"Robbie. Robbie," she moaned. I rubbed her cold hands, trying to get the blood flowing. "I imagined so many things," she told me. "I kept thinking he'd used his cash machine card, and someone shot him for the money. I imagined so many terrible things."

We both knew the reality was far too horrible to have ever considered. I held my mother, who felt very old and frail, at barely sixty-seven. I could not let my tears come; not yet.

"I want to see Charlene and the kids," I whispered. I had to get out of the chaos of my mother's home, where everyone talked at cross purposes. They wanted to help. Several women offered to drive me back to Virginia to pick up my car, though I had just arrived.

Inside my brother's home—yes, it was still his home—a quiet subdued grief was a nearly welcome relief from all the talk of what should be done. All of us who deeply loved Robert needed time to accept that very little could be done anymore. Except simple things, like helping my nine-year-old nephew Justin cut and toast a bagel or reading a story to Jenna, a few years younger and seemingly unaware of what she had just lost.

Charlene, impeccable even ravaged by grief, barely moved from her spot on the sofa. That day was, would have been, their twelfth wedding anniversary. "Why?" my sister-in-law moaned. "Why today?" They had dinner reservations for the prior evening and her parents were to watch the kids. But Robert was missing.

Not knowing any words that might soothe her, I just held her and stroked her back. How would she go on? How do you move past something like this?

I thought of Dick, who I had untangled from in bed barely hours earlier, sitting in the courtroom covering the Mayor Barry trial for AP. He knew nothing. I left a message with a news clerk, and my tentative boyfriend of six months quickly called me back.

I told him what had happened.

"What can I do?" he asked in a warm embracing tone.

"I have to get home tonight and I don't have my car."

"Give me your brother's address."

As evening came, the home filled with Robert's many long-time friends. That quirky Jewish humor was everywhere, even in such a horrible moment. I hadn't seen many of those people for years and remarked absently to one of his friends still single. "Will we ever get married, Brian?"

"We will get married, Susan, but probably not to each other." For some odd reason, I found that very funny. My hangover was fast morphing into a migraine.

Robert's friend Sandy was taking some people to the funeral home to say goodbye. My mother asked me if I wanted to go.

"No." I would have to talk to Robert if I went, and I wasn't ready. I felt only shock, was totally devoid of any feelings to be expressed. How could I look at my brother's prone, lifeless form and say anything that might bring him back?

Dad and Shirley were traveling and would not disembark the ship until late that night. We had to delay the funeral an additional day. Slowly, we worked out details.

"Someone is here to see you, Susan."

I went to the door and found Dick, holding flowers. Before I could explain about the taboo, someone slipped past and kindly took the bouquet and put the stems in a vase. As a Northern Baptist,

Dick had no way of knowing. He'd brought something beautiful, fleetingly so. I prefer to believe the essence of one's spirit never wilts. I am sometimes sorry I did not visit Robert's body, to at least have given him one last kiss. Instead, I have had all these years to imagine him only as vibrant. It is a rare day when I do not speak to him. He answers me, if I listen closely.

CHAPTER 5

Hindsight can be as vividly deceptive as a painted clown: everything is exaggerated except for the crucial details hidden in the folded recesses of memory. How hard it is to siphon through and discover things I have long overlooked. My brother's life was seemingly filled with solid friendships and enormous love. Only by expanding the parameters do I get an inkling of what I was missing, and what blinded me to so much that did not fall under the purview of my own rollicking life.

My name appeared on the *Rolling Stone* masthead under "Editorial Staff" early in 1977, right there in alphabetical order with Iris Brown, Michael Duffey, Lyssa Waters, and the San Francisco cadre that would not be traveling east to New York with the editors, writers, and production people when the big move occurred that summer.

Not everyone cheered this massive relocation. While the

magazine's founder, Jann Wenner, and his business team saw gold in Manhattan's skyline, the original editors and writers viewed leaving San Francisco as the collapse of civilization.

As for me, the move opened up a job—and a world—that far exceeded my hopes and dreams. Despite some quivering trepidation over being music illiterate, I blundered in with enough energy and enthusiasm to compensate for my shortcomings. Only in a newsroom jammed with oversized personalities and every form of altered consciousness could I have pulled this off.

Iris stationed me in the large central alcove of the New York annex, where I was to guard the front door while carrying out my miscellaneous tasks. This put me smack in the center of all the magazine activity. One new editor who started around that same time admitted to me that he thought of my position as formidable, believing he had to win my favor to get anywhere at *Rolling Stone*. I set him straight, being no more than a glorified receptionist. Usually people did not knock; instead, they barged unannounced through unlocked doors and either knew where they were going or caught my attention long enough for me to guide them. Many people stopped to chat, allowing me to quickly get to know these outrageous music critics, political feature writers, and miscellaneous music industry personalities.

As the comings and goings were sporadic in the small annex, I could easily turn my back to the entry when setting up the Mojo wire to send copy to San Francisco or receive a burst of pages from Hunter Thompson. By dubbing it the "Mojo wire," Hunter gave this primitive fax some pizazz. Strip the nomenclature away and the machine was nothing more than a rotating cylinder that took nearly ten minutes to transmit a page and stunk like burnt ink. The Mojo wire sounded like driving on a blown tire, so loud that I could ignore the irritating Dylanesque parody coming from the doorway behind me. Someone was singing off-key about knocking on heaven's door. After a moment or two of listening to this singing, I looked over my shoulder and froze.

The round ball of energy serenading me at the door was

unmistakable. Scruffy hair falling around blue eyes, otherwise preppy with laundered jeans and leather loafers, a telltale brown cigarillo gripped in short thick fingers. As I pushed open the door, his song ended, and the Mojo finished another page. Through a toothy smile, he blurted, "Hi, I'm Jann Wenner. I own this magazine."

I sputtered my name.

But his attention had already shifted to someone else. "I've got something for you," he yelled to the back of a writer's head before beelining down the hall screaming for Iris.

An expletive shot from my mouth. That was not how I wanted to meet Jann Wenner—me being caught off guard and reduced to a blabbering fool.

Charles Young, a.k.a. Reverend Charles M. Young, or simply Chuck, looked up and shrugged at me through the plate glass that separated his cubicle office from my desk. The rising star Random Notes editor had recently graduated from Columbia Journalism School in the same class as Lyssa, who shared my lowly spot on the masthead. Her main responsibility was to ensure that freelancers got paid. Chuck wrote cover stories.

It took a certain steel-bristled woman to succeed in the mid-1970s workplace. Many did develop biting edges at *Rolling Stone* and scramble up the ranks. But Lyssa could never get her feet dug into the slippery slide of that chaos, despite her talent.

Lyssa's male counterpart, Michael Duffey, worked with her on compiling reader's comments and polling results when he wasn't fact-checking articles on deadline. He also contributed to the Random Notes column on a regular basis by collecting quotes from rockers at nightclubs.

Chuck and Michael emerged from their cubicles to laugh at my distress. They looked nearly alike, with round wire-rimmed glasses that magnified strained blue eyes. Both wore wrinkled Oxford shirts and washed-out jeans.

"You've met the *man*," Chuck said.

"I would have preferred a nicer introduction," I said, but I laughed with them anyway.

"Want tickets to see Southside Johnny at the Bottom Line?" Chuck asked me. Industry flacks often contacted him with press invites.

"Can I write a Random Note?"

"If you hear something worth writing."

I had been at the magazine for just over a month and had already learned I would have to be well positioned to grab a good quote. The crush of reporters had nearly knocked me over on a recent excursion with Michael to the Bottom Line to see Elvis Costello.

"Push them aside," Michael had yelled to me, "You've got a *Rolling Stone* press pass."

I'd fought my way through until I was face to face with the singer, who had me directly in his sight lines behind his trademark black-rimmed glasses.

"Ask a question," Michael prodded.

In a shaky voice, I had asked, "Can you tell me the genesis of any songs on your new album*?*"

Elvis just stared at me.

Michael leaped forward, playing tag team. He held a pen and pad firmly. "Elvis, we're from *Rolling Stone.* We'd like to know who might have been the role model for Alison."

"A cashier at a local supermarket," the singer answered. "She had a face that could have launched ships."

Our one-minute with Elvis was up and Michael, kind Michael, had pulled me from disgrace. His save allowed me to retreat through the press horde without being the butt of ridicule. And we—well, Michael—had grabbed a printable quote.

◆   ◆   ◆

This glittering rock world I had plunged into could not blot out everything. By late February I had an urge to see Robert in

Baltimore. We had been together briefly at Dad and Shirley's house in Harrisburg during the holidays, but I wanted to see him alone. Just a hunch, a sibling sense, but something gnawed at me. Too many odd occurrences had linked together and set off an alarm. A much-younger Robert had experienced a string of accidents: blowing the wrong way on a pipe full of pool chemicals as a summer lifeguard; being attacked by a dog who may or may not have been provoked; and, a strange fall from a broken deck as many watched. These were incidents that happened in quick succession then stopped. He somehow resumed perfect control of his life, and it became too easy for all of us to forget these incidents had occurred.

Now in his midtwenties, Robert's emotional tumbles over the past couple years strung together as heavy weights on my heart. He'd broken up with Faye, the beautiful Greek-American girl whom he had dated since before college. It happened so suddenly and, it appeared, somewhat irrationally. She adored him. I thought their bond welded tighter than steel, until the day Robert snapped the relationship apart. He never said why. Then my brother dropped out of the University of Maryland with only a few credits remaining to receive his undergraduate degree. He ran intellectual circles around his friends. They would be the first to admit that. Robert wrote papers for Ducky, who became a lawyer; tutored Sandy in math so he could get into medical school; and coaxed Harold through courses to prepare him to become a CPA at a big downtown accounting firm. Yet Robert left College Park without any real prospects.

Uncle Morty hired him at the Apollo shirt factory to run the floor and make sure all the ladies at the sewing machines kept to their quotas. Apollo was an Offermann family business. Morty and his brother, Saul, worked for their dad. And now Robert, who was in no way an Offermann, worked for a man who had married our Aunt Shifra. Robert was only family by marriage, a very loose connection for a clan as insular and proud as the Offermanns. He took a dead-end job; we all knew it but said nothing.

Robert and his close friend, Harold, were bunking in the small house on Milford Mill Road in Baltimore that was vacated when Dad and Shirley moved to Harrisburg. That was where I went to see Robert, when I took the train to Baltimore because of this hunch, because of the string of things that formed a row of question marks. Those events had occurred over time, but they bundled together in my mind because of our physical distance. My brother had come back to Baltimore. I was many miles gone.

How odd it was for me to knock on the door where I had spent so many Sunday afternoons during childhood, in the post-Vagabond years. With Shirley being such an excellent cook, the house always smelled of something wonderful. Now aromas like pungent barbeque ribs marinating and cooking for hours were only a distant memory. Robert and Harold filled the house with old furniture too large for the space and soiled athletic gear. I'm not sure they ever turned on the oven.

Robert sat in one of those oversized chairs and surveyed me. "You look good," he said.

I patted my hips. "I haven't lost the weight I gained in Europe."

"You needed those pounds."

Robert still saw me as that wisp of a girl, generally invisible as his large personality dominated our family and social circles in those years of growing up. He did not want to see that I had become an adult, preferring, no doubt, his memories of the skinny kid who idolized her big brother. My very first words after crawling into his empty bedroom were, "Where Baba?"

"You look good too." He did. He looked great, especially when that magnetic smile lit up his face. I caught a glimpse or two of the shadows taking over his features, but the darkness never lasted for more than a fleeting moment. I could almost overlook it.

"How's Mom? Ted?" he asked since I was staying with them during my short weekend visit.

"They're fine. Hard to believe Mom finally remarried." Ted Patz was fifteen years older than our mother, but he had stature as an advertising executive. They bought a townhouse and Mrs. Annette Patz went all out with decorating. And Grandma Rose, who'd kept the apartment, could have her friends over for canasta whenever she pleased.

Robert asked about *Rolling Stone.* "Wow, my little sister at a big-time magazine. I'm really proud of you." And he was; I could hear it in his voice. Robert was genuinely happy to see me thriving in New York City.

With him, I felt only a small twinge to have landed such an exciting job. I wished that Robert had pursued something big too. He had been the one with exceptional promise. Not me. But I could not delve deep enough that day. I never asked him what I should have: *What is holding you back?*

Instead, I let Robert ask the questions, starting with my apartment, and I prattled on about the sublease I'd signed with two roommates on the Upper East Side shortly after the women's film festival had put some money in my pocket in October. I made Robert laugh, telling him how I shared the apartment with a beautiful young Jamaican woman who had been married with a child, but left her family to work in the city. "She taught me how cocoa butter smoothed over the belly through and after pregnancy will preserve your original body sculpture."

"That might become valuable information for you at some point," he said. It was a gentle nudge to remind me that I might one day have a family.

My other roomie was French Algerian, I told him, and worked as a beautician with Vidal Sassoon. The man himself had cut her hair into his signature pixie, which framed her huge brown eyes and long flared nose. Both girls tutored me nonstop on how to attract men—rich men—by getting myself a hairstyle and some glitzy clothes. "It's so tedious."

"Don't you want to attract a rich man? Make Mom happy?"

I had so much more to do. "I need to establish myself at the magazine."

A shadow crossed his face again; I added, "Perhaps one day I'll settle down." My brother could never bear to see me alone, miles and eons from his protection.

"But you'll never come back to Baltimore. Not you." Said with a brother's understanding of his sister. Said with some sadness.

We were headed at lightning speed in different directions. I tried to grasp at something. "I don't have the pack of friends here that you have. I don't love the Orioles. And I don't even understand football." Every Sunday afternoon when Robert would sit with Dad and watch the Baltimore Colts, I would wander to a nearby park and jump from one giant rock to another.

"This is *my* city," he proudly said.

"I'll always know where to find you." Those words made sense, then; now, I realize it was only wishful thinking.

◆　◆　◆

How easily other things distracted me from Robert.

I had never met investigative journalist Howard Kohn but very much respected his articles, especially the series on Karen Silkwood. I went out of my way to send pertinent clips to him in San Francisco via the interoffice mail pouch. Howard's priorities quickly began to take precedence over the reporters' needs in the New York annex. My taking a shine to Howard must have been detected. Shortly before my three-month mark, Iris asked to talk to me.

A nomad of Manhattan's streets, Iris always dressed for mobility in petite-sized black jeans, a baseball jacket, and sneakers. She carried a satchel with a change of clothing into the office, and out again, on the days that she actually made it to work. I got a glimpse of her world when she would take me with her through the fluid urban maze. Starting in the center with cocaine lines, our feet on the sidewalk would take us in ever-widening circles, often meeting up with people along the way, drinking bottles of wine, talking. There exists in Midtown, probably even today, a Japanese restaurant where we would often conclude the evening with bowls of noodle soup. I could recall the miso and scallion fragrances of the meal in the morning, but never the location. When I found myself lost inside that maze again, I always had to follow Iris out. I was very intrigued with her, and maybe a little in love.

Iris was an entirely different person in the office. The epitome of efficiency, she was a legend for her quicksilver typing skills and instant recall of names and numbers. Jann would have been lost without her. She was so good that her unexplained absences were never questioned. When she called me into her office, I knew this was not for a fun chat. Her unruly black hair would always be captured in a tight bun when she intended to be serious. Her face never gave away secrets. Heavy-lidded eyes darkly glowed above her cheekbones and a perky smile even when I could see the extra makeup she wore to erase any signs of being up all night. She was a striking beauty; many called her exotic.

In her office next to Lyssa, who could hear things that were not even said, Iris shut the door before she spoke. "Are you enjoying the job?"

Not wanting to appear too effusive, I simply responded, "Sure."

"Good. Good." She glanced at some notes on her desk and pulled a menthol cigarette from a crinkled package. She offered me one.

Still rolling my own cigarettes, I was happy to accept her ready-made. It took Iris time to reveal exactly what she had to say. I had no choice but to let her set the pace.

"We're in the process of deciding how to organize the new office after the San Francisco people are here." She paused. "You seem to like helping out our political writers."

I had done nothing to hide my preference for the hard-core politicos over those who were making and breaking rock stars. Joe

Klein was a big deal in the New York office when I got there, and he was doing great pieces, everything from a cover profile of Jimmy Carter's whiz kids—Hamilton Jordan and Jody Powell—to an early sketch of the life of Woody Guthrie that would become a full-length book. Though short in stature, Joe gave *Rolling Stone* heft in the political arena. He asked a lot of me in the two years we worked together, constantly relying on my assistance, but he gave back in solid pointers. He taught me the basic rules of news reporting, drilled them into me. His cantankerousness prepared me for what lay ahead when I sought a career in straight journalism.

Iris said the new seating arrangement had me sitting right outside the office of the News & Opinions editor, a distinguished writer named Gloria Emerson who would shortly join the magazine.

"You'll like her," Iris said.

My phone-answering responsibilities would be taken over by a receptionist-office manager who was moving to New York with the San Francisco crew. All this sounded very good to me.

"Just one thing," she continued. "I'm just saying this as a friend now. But I think you should really bone up on the music scene and show more interest in emerging bands. That would be your real opportunity for promotion. Spend more time at the music clubs," Iris advised.

"I can do that."

I had to. Just recently, when Iris had not shown up at work, Jann ordered me to take dictation on a letter and then type it up. Fast. My shorthand nonexistent, I'd struggled to jot Jann's words in a steno book, too nervous to ask him to repeat anything.

"I need that pronto," he'd yelled as I trotted out of his office.

The revolving ball on my electric typewriter never moved so fast. I typed from memory more than from my scrawled words. But I made mistakes. Some I could fix through the whiteout ribbon on the machine, but I wanted it to look perfect. I retyped it.

Jann stood behind me as I was finishing and barked, "I expected that letter a half hour ago."

"It's done." I slid the sheet from the machine.

He grabbed the letter and read it fast. "It's all right, but you're very slow. Not exactly a typist, are you?"

I had to agree.

He'd turned to leave. "We'll have to find something else for you to do."

My options were narrowing fast. If I wanted to stay at the magazine, I would have to throw myself into music. Not just go to concerts, not just fight my way through reporters, but also make sense of the songs I had heard.

I called Robert that night very upset.

"I'm not sure how to get more into the music," I told him after I relayed my conversation with Iris. "How do I show them I've got the stuff to be a music writer?"

"Let the music take you."

"Take me where?"

"You'll just have to trust the music."

I could picture him as we spoke: those deep-set, nearly black eyes, rich dark hair with enough facial growth even after shaving to shadow everything but his overwhelming smile.

"Trust the music?" I questioned.

"If you want to be a music writer Susan, you're just going to have to listen harder, interpret, follow the music."

"Follow it?"

"Yes," he said, "but don't fall down the rabbit hole."

How I appreciated my brother's humorous advice, always turning to him when in doubt or distress. But such guidance was one-way. He never revealed his conflicts or emotional needs to me or, as far as I know, to anyone else. Whenever I questioned him about anything to do with his life, he spoke only in positive terms. I have no memories of him being down, not since childhood when his wounds were still raw, and he had not yet developed the ability to deftly hide his feelings. I never learned how to call his bluff. He was too agile, too clever, too able to deflect any attempt to learn what was going on behind that bright smile.

CHAPTER 6

Jayne Loader and I barreled down the avenues of Manhattan with everything we owned flapping in the back of a borrowed truck. My film historian-writer friend finally convinced me to move downtown. I had loosely tied my clothes that morning in sheets and taped my boxes of books until the edges shone with cellophane. My small Olivetti typewriter snapped shut like luggage next to me in the front seat. Behind us, I could see nothing except our flailing detritus in the pit of the truck bed, and upper Manhattan vanishing.

Jayne had retrieved her possessions from storage at a friend's farm in Connecticut and borrowed their family truck, a vehicle generally used to haul garbage to the local dump. We drove through urban streets with the muffler kicking like a gunshot.

"No more views of the East River or coffee from my favorite Greeks," I sighed. Not sad, wistful.

"Good riddance," Jayne blurted as we crossed to the west side through a Central Park vibrantly alive in April greenery.

I thought of the doorman, also gone. But who needs an elevator and a doorman? Products of a capitalist society, like air conditioning, mopped floors, and working heat. None of that would await us in Chelsea. My new neighborhood spanned blocks of mostly rent-controlled apartments in old brownstones that hid immigrant families among the gamut of artists, writers, and musicians cycling through, most notably in the landmark Chelsea Hotel. We had found a top-floor apartment in a brownstone with a view over the Hudson River to New Jersey. *Hoboken Welcomes Industry* screamed the huge sign visible from our kitchen window. Called a two bedroom, one of the sleeping quarters served as an anteroom to the bathroom. Kitchen-dining-living space forged a compact unit with windows opening in the back to a fire escape. Five narrow flights up, and we loved the apartment for its bare charm and absence of pretension.

Moving day brought out my *Rolling Stone* colleagues to help carry the load. Lyssa, her wild blond hair pulled into two tight braids, sat on the front steps as we arrived. She had already gone up and, as I would later see, quietly placed a small potted plant in the bare kitchen, an action so unlike her that the small, barely noticeable bloom truly touched me. Lyssa disappeared early that day without saying goodbye. I knew her being there at all took considerable effort. She was awkward with people, never fully comfortable. I can only imagine how difficult it must have been for her to work at the collision course that was *Rolling Stone*.

The others began to arrive. Michael Duffey and Chuck Young came dressed in muscle shirts and shorts, ready for heavy lifting. Country music editor Chet Flippo came too, his Cheshire cat smile bright enough to illuminate the dark, daring neighborhood that was now my home. At least I could see past the fire escapes, past Tenth Avenue, to where the Hudson River ran.

The guys sang as they rounded each corner to conquer another flight of stairs with loads on their backs and bags in their arms.

What shall we do with a drunken sailor?
What shall we do with a drunken sailor?
Early in the morning?

Upstairs, Chet immediately pored through Jayne's records, either nodding approvingly or shaking his head with his thumb held downward. Delbert McClinton, vigorous approval; Iggy Pop, grunt. Jayne argued that Dolly Parton, subject of Chet's recent amorous cover story, lacked the singing talent that he'd purported. Little argument ensued, as Chet never pretended his true admiration for Dolly extended as high as her vocal cords.

Paul Scanlon had promised to come, and I hoped that he would. But I really only anticipated an excuse mumbled to me on Monday morning on what might have deterred him. I never expected anything, as the gossamer feel of things between us could so easily unravel. Although sexual overtures among staff could be heard even above the music blaring from critics' alcoves, my first foray into that intimate camaraderie, with a senior editor, had caught me off guard.

A month earlier, the publicists at 20th Century Fox had set up a preview of *Star Wars* in a private viewing room for *Rolling Stone*'s New York staff. Paul sat beside me in the dark as John Williams' movie score drowned out everything else and took us to a galaxy far, far away. By the time Harrison Ford, in a John Wayne stance, muttered, "I've been from one end of this galaxy to another, kid," I'd fallen against Paul's warm shoulder, his hand spread-eagled on my knee. The movie left me breathless. I couldn't board a subway uptown after being taken on such a wild ride in space with fingertips roaming across my thighs during the light laser fights. I needed to talk robots, at the very least.

Paul suggested a drink at Maggie's Pub in Gramercy Park. I knew Paul lived in an apartment right off the park and was agreeable.

Maggie's offered old-world ambiance, not swept clean of its rough-hewn surface like so many Manhattan bars. Paul ordered an Irish whisky. I asked for the same, though I hadn't cultivated a palate for fine blends. He cringed when I poured in water, but it lightened the amber and made my double easier to down. He ordered us another round.

I felt my cheeks turning the pinched pink of dime-store blush. His dark-fringed eyes lowering toward my face made me self-conscious. He kissed me then, and again as we walked toward his apartment. On a March evening, the winds off the East River blew cool enough for us to seek the warmth of each other.

Watching Paul arrive in Chelsea on moving day with his sleeves rolled up and willing to help out only strengthened my resolve that living downtown was the right decision, despite my mother's concerns.

Robert had told me that Mom was terrified of me living in a building without a doorman. "You know how she is." Our mother's neurotic kvetches were something else that bound us tight. My mother depended on Robert; she always had. She would call him whenever I was five minutes late returning home or, as time passed, if she couldn't reach me at college or in New York. And I always depended on Robert to placate her.

Paul came bearing a bottle of Jack Daniels. "Which is your apartment?"

Everyone pointed upward.

"A climb?"

"But worth every step," Jayne yelled as she propped open the door.

Way-hay, up she rises
Way-hay, up she rises

We eventually got everything upstairs and someone suggested going up on the roof. Viewing the Manhattan landscape from the tarmac height revealed a different world. With doors and windows barricaded, New York City is mostly sealed. Rooftops liberate by providing a panorama vista of living, breathing spaces.

We watched the sun set behind the Chrysler Building, all of us inebriated on Jack Daniels as lights illuminated the Empire State Building. Chet left early to return home to his wife, but the others stayed. Chuck was caught in conversation with Jayne, whose Texas drawl grew more elongated with the bourbon. I had never seen Chuck laugh so loudly at someone else's remarks, as he preferred to be the wit. I talked to Michael and Paul until my young colleague left to meet up with his friends at a nightclub, leaving me alone with Paul.

I liked the informal Paul. Stripped of his professional jeans and button-up shirt, he seemed more on my level. Never once had he indicated that something might be developing between us. And he didn't that night either.

He did ask, "Do you have something to sleep on tonight?"

"Nothing comfortable." I met his warm brown gaze. The platform bed I had ordered at the woodworkers' shop on Eighth Avenue would be delivered Monday, I told him.

Jayne had already spirited Chuck back into the apartment. They would have to be the ones to inaugurate this Chelsea space and exorcise the ghosts of those who had climbed those five flights in the past.

Paul took me back to Gramercy Park, where we watched science fiction films on TV, and I lingered one more night in his bed and arms. Sex with him continued its silken feel. I particularly liked the way he stroked back my hair to better view my face. "You are lovely," he said. I sensed that he was comparing me with someone else. If I was *lovely*, perhaps she was *beautiful*.

Paul never ended our brief affair. To articulate why our worlds must separate would generate negative energy that neither of us wanted. The rules of the newsroom permitted fleeting sex if, afterward, it's unhooked like a catch-and-release fish. I had to learn to live within this system, as I had to learn to live in Chelsea.

CHAPTER 7

Eventually the tarmac roof, my platform over Manhattan, collected the summer sun and turned the apartment into a small hell. I missed Paul, even though I saw him nearly every day in the office and drank with him most nights at Wilde's Tavern, where we all gathered when the workday ended. Later, home alone in Chelsea, the day's accumulated heat would throw me into an inebriated torpor. With Jayne mostly on the road, the quiet could sometimes be deafening. I often left the warm apartment and walked down Ninth Avenue to Fourteenth Street, crossed into the West Village, strolled around Washington Square Park, and went inside the Strand bookstore with its miles of stacks. I usually walked back a different route, just to breathe in another part of the city.

I had traveled throughout much of Europe before landing in Manhattan. But this city to me embraced the entire world in its potpourri of foods, accents, arts, and universal colors. Street vendors kept hot foods turning on spits and charred meaty smells kept me perpetually hungry. All of my senses awoke there.

In reality, the city I loved faced bankruptcy, soaring crime rates, mechanical failures, and decaying garbage. Yet the sewer smells in parts of the West Village recalled Italy for me and I would sit happily at outside cafes with my journal and wine, blind to everything except for the activity of the immediate street scene. I somehow never took in the city's blight. Those streets were my escape and, as I walked, I felt at one with the whizzing-by sirens, the homeless, the storefronts, and those who gathered on stoops.

At my lowest points, I believed that what was rotting was myself. Old wounds fester, like the scars cut by the edge of my mother's voice when she refused to let us see our father until he paid child support. Robert would be pounding his fist into his catchers' glove, softening the leather, preparing to stand on the bleachers at Memorial Stadium to catch a fly ball. Dad would arrive. There would be words. Later I would see Robert's unused glove flung in a corner.

Loneliness and sadness could creep in like an unwelcome visitor anywhere. My world had come vibrantly alive in New York City. Even so, there were crushing moments when I had to walk fast to keep old demons at bay. Falling from the ecstatic heights of the music world to the painful pits of my past in a matter of an hour or two meant an inevitable crash landing. I often tried splashing the heavy ache away with bottles of wine.

"Does it ever haunt you?" I called Robert one night to ask. "All that ugly talk about Dad? Years of fighting?"

"No," he said firmly, "not at all. And it shouldn't bother you either. What's past is past." His constant refrain: "Let it go."

How could he compartmentalize those emotions? I envied him that, then. Later I would learn the real dangers of stuffing emotional pain in a dank drawer like old socks. Hidden things fester. I took a very different approach: actively living with my demons, albeit through many raucous, wild, nearly destructive rides, but always hanging on for dear life.

At a certain point, I knew it was time to do something other than drown myself in drink. I started running. Trotting slowly in old tennis shoes toward the World Trade Centers, I caught glimpses of myself in storefront windows on Wall Street looking less-than-gazelle-like in torn tights and blousy T-shirts. I stretched exactly how I had been told, arms arced and hips twisting my body into a sharp U, then toe touching, reaching for the sky, and down again. The entire concept of jogging struck me as comical until I slowly caught the rhythm and began enjoying the feel of my shoe rubber on the roads and sidewalks.

Running gave me time to think about what I really wanted at the job, thoughts often ambling toward what I seemed unable to accomplish. My uncritical ear refused to sift through musical chords with any point of reference. It was impossible for me to distinguish a good guitar solo from an outstanding musical feat. Despite going to many concerts and clubs, any distinctive new sounds—ones I might attempt to write about—filtered through my ears into jumbled noise. What words could communicate formless sound? What I enjoyed were the simple instruments like wooden spoons and fiddles that a group of ad hoc musicians brought on Wednesday nights to a bar in the Meatpacking District. Most of the meatpackers worked at night and drank in the mornings, leaving the neighborhood's bars largely empty in the evenings. I could easily walk the few blocks from Chelsea and feel part of the rustic music that filled the meatpackers' space once or twice a week. Occasionally I would be given a set of spoons to clang and clatter. If only I could write about this colorful collection of individuals with their handmade instruments. But I never did. Such a down-home rustic piece would never be published in *Rolling Stone*. Besides, these escapes were my own—private, like the running.

Nothing to keep me in bed on Saturday mornings, I got up early and ran the old West Side highway to Battery Park City with other joggers who appreciated that urban planning dragged on for years, since it would be the late eighties before the city transformed the old infrastructure. Yet the abandoned highway gave runners perfect views of the Hudson River and no cars or trucks on the same lateral to pass fumes. I'd swing by the small corner grocery on the return trip and pick up warm bagels.

"The best thing you ever did was start running," Jayne would say when she smelled the fresh bread, though she was barely awake as I turned on the coffee maker.

Our dining area consisted of a high Formica counter just long enough for two plates and our accumulated clutter. High bar stools provided seating at the counter to eat our crusty, soft-centered classic New York bagels with schmears of cream cheese.

I reminded Jayne that several of us were catching a new act at the Bottom Line, meeting for drinks first at Max's Kansas City, a Warhol haunt recently reopened under new ownership and with an entirely different crowd. Andy Warhol would not mingle with the disco set that now frequented the lower Park Avenue address. Chuck had invited Jayne as his plus-one.

"Right, I'm looking forward to that," Jayne said. I could nearly follow her mind's machinations by watching her face transform. I wasn't totally surprised when she blurted, "Have you ever thought about becoming monogamous?"

"Jayne," I started, "how can I become monogamous when I'm practically celibate?"

"Come on, it hasn't been that long since you and Paul. You've mentioned flirting with some guys."

"The last night I spent with Paul was the night we moved in here, many weeks ago. And flirting isn't action. Nearly every guy at *Rolling Stone* flirts with me. Doesn't mean anything except that I work in a very horny, very heterosexual office."

That I could blot out what was occurring all around me—how many people at *Rolling Stone* were, in fact, dabbling with bisexuality—

never altered the tempo of our conversation. I only pause now, as I'm struck by the blinders that I wore. Not being cognizant of my colleagues' sexual proclivities or drug habits is one thing. How much I didn't see with Robert is the lingering ache.

Where was Robert that Saturday morning in 1977? What was he doing as I sat in that Chelsea kitchen talking to Jayne? It was so easy to simply imagine him out with the in-crowd, still that shining star at its center. But other things were going on with my brother, underemployed in Uncle Morty's shirt factory while nearly everyone else he knew was carving out prosperous lives in the Baltimore suburbs. As I would soon learn, he was doing something bound to have dangerous repercussions. I had no way of knowing, as the Robert I spoke to on the phone expounded only on fun times.

"Hypothetically," Jayne persisted, "would you ever choose to be monogamous?"

"Maybe." I did believe in forever love.

"You think monogamy might be worth an experiment, at some point?"

"Yeah, sure." How I wanted to be enraptured by one terrific man, but something edgy—and afraid—inside my psyche would not allow that to happen. Everyone thought I would marry my college boyfriend, yet before graduation I found a way to whittle out of our cohabitated relationship.

Our exchange amused me later as we ordered another round of drinks at Max's and I watched Jayne jealously eying all the female rockers and groupies that came by to chat up Chuck, whose dramatic flair and graphic writing style had turned him into a real rock personality. Even sitting there as Chuck's escort, I knew she was thinking about some new guy she'd recently met. Jayne had told me a few things about this filmmaker she interviewed in Virginia. Monogamy was a funny word to come out of her mouth. She could keep me up half the night with stories about boyfriends scattered across the country.

We sat in a deep wooden booth with high slats separating us from the main bar area. Suddenly an arm circled by a heavy rawhide-studded bracelet shot through the slats, thumb up and index finger pointed at Chuck. Her hissing sounded like arrows flying past.

The Runaways' Cherie Currie, trailed by rhythm guitarist Joan Jett, had good reason to pummel Chuck. He had written a cover story the previous October on the Runaways for *Crawdaddy,* describing how Cherie asked him for a sheet of paper from his steno pad to stuff in the crotch of her red jumpsuit. "My skin is allergic to the metal in zippers," she'd told him. "I can't dance when I itch." As revealed in his article, he had suggested she autograph the paper for him after the practice session.

Jayne leaned in, amused by the drama. Cameras flashed. Rock photographer Richard Aarons captured the scene in black and white. Cherie's rawhide wrath inches from the silk bandana I had sleekly wrapped around my forehead. I wore a dress from a vintage clothing store on Second Avenue that sparkled in the bar lights, my slight smile disarmingly innocent.

All's fair in rock journalism, Chuck explained to Cherie. Nothing is too foul to print, and performers more than provided the fodder for his outrageous portrayals. "I write no lies," he insisted.

Cherie and Joan offered only a weak defense. Any press, even sleazy, beat out no press, which equaled no presence. As an all-female rock band comprised of teenagers and a newly released album, the Runaways needed ink splatters. Lewdness put them in the cherished limelight with the song "Cherry Bomb" as their big hit.

We all drank too much that night and partied until two or three in the morning. Jayne stayed at Chuck's place on the Upper West Side and, alone, I slept in on a rainy Sunday morning until noon and then watched old movies on my eight-inch black-and-white television.

Dreary days were always good for calling my mother, who unfailingly picked up on the third ring.

"Yes," she said. "Hello" would have been too accepting. My mother would remain skeptical of the telephone until the day she died.

Once she knew it was me, her tone changed. "Hi, sweetie. I was just thinking about you."

"Good thoughts, I hope."

"I was thinking about how you never call me."

"Life is busy," I said. "Hey, I met the Runaways last night."

"That's nice."

She wanted me to tell her how I had been swept off my feet by a Wall Street lawyer. But that would never happen.

"Robert is doing well," she told me. "He's talking about going to night school to finish the college credits he needs to graduate. That would be so good."

Robert would always tell our mother exactly what she wanted to hear. And she believed him. My first frat party in high school would absolutely have no alcohol. He would watch out for me. No guy would dare kiss me with Robert hovering close. Lie. Lie. Lie. He'd advised me quietly to drink a large glass of milk before my date came and to repeat nothing that I saw or experienced, on pain of death. The latter was no problem. I had retained no memory of anything after my third or fourth shot of Southern Comfort.

No reason to shower or dress that Sunday until it was time to go out again. Shower is a misnomer. The tub in our fifth-floor walkup stood on four porcelain feet but had no elevated water projectile. A rubber hose and nozzle from the bath faucet could wet and rinse my hair, requiring dexterity to keep water in the tub. In the end, I was clean, or clean enough for a city where the garbage sat on the street for weeks, Son of Sam roamed, and more dangers always lurked.

CHAPTER 8

Using city ingenuity, our Chelsea walkup on West Twenty-Second Street became home. Jayne taught me how to wander the streets on garbage day to discover treasures among the trash. A discarded narrow wooden cabinet the same height as the kitchen counter would hold the telephone and a few dishes. Old frames could be refurbished with new prints bought on sale at museum gift shops. One store on Eighth Avenue charged only ten dollars to deliver a second-hand wooden armoire up the flights of steps strapped to the back of the store's owner. A black-and-white houndstooth sofa bed came courtesy of a cousin.

Once we had accumulated enough seating—about a month or so after the big move—I invited the *Rolling Stone* crowd over for Jayne's Texas Chili to show our gratitude for the brawn extended on moving day. Getting kitchenware to serve the food proved the fun part since a Pottery Barn outlet took up nearly an entire block on Tenth Avenue, directly across from the Empire Diner and only a half block from us. After several trips back and forth, I bought enough plates and glasses for a crowd, and a glazed brown pot large enough for Jayne to create her culinary work of art.

Smells of browned ground beef, cumin, and loads of chili pepper wafted down five flights and met us at the entry as we reached Chelsea from the *Rolling Stone* office in time for dinner. Jayne stood aproned to pull aside the door and let us in with our bags of beer and wine. Chuck, still smitten with Jayne, brought champagne. Chet, another native Texan, looked radiantly transported to native soil at the sight of dried chili peppers that Jayne had found at the outdoor fruit and vegetable market. Turns out that both Texans hailed from Fort Worth and Jayne quickly ran through the litany of cultural icons that bound her with Chet to a time and place, they both agreed, probably better left behind. Michael and Lyssa staked out the sofa, while the rest of us drank beer a few yards away in the kitchen alcove. I had invited Paul, but he never came.

I liked my tight New York pack, particularly Michael. With no illusions of ever becoming a famous rock critic, he did his job without elbowing others. Chet also became a real friend; his office door always open to me. Chuck and Lyssa kept their journalism-school edge: his effectively sharp; hers more subdued, despite her recent success in getting a byline in *Ms.* magazine.

Looking across the room in the late-day glow, all the pieces came together: the cast-off sofa, iron window bars, items hauled from the heap, new dishes, and a wooden coffee table found in a store window. As though a paintbrush had put a coat of caramel varnish over the whole shebang, the apartment took on a cooked-in shiny personality that made me feel I had a real home for the first time.

I never had the space growing up in a small apartment to spill out my confused adolescent emotions. Robert kept his bedroom door clicked shut, even to me, especially to me. Beatles songs wafted out;

eventually his musical tastes turned eerily psychedelic, replays of "In-a-Gadda-da-Vida" reverberating through tightly wrapped bed covers in the room I shared with my mother. Now, finally, in the golden glow of Chelsea, I could slowly unravel myself.

During much solo stomping through the East and West Village, and many more hours of running the elevated West Highway and Central Park, I slowly began to confront the baggage left from the growing-up world I had escaped. Some of it opened easily, like the tensions over money and my father's crimes. Locked away was the absence of emotional support when the only world we knew disintegrated in an instant. We did not see Dad for so very long. Only many years later would I understand how I detrimentally patterned my life—by resisting true intimacy with men—to avoid such a painful loss again.

Robert internalized those early experiences in a far more destructive way. He acted as if he harbored no residue from our early childhood, laughed at me if I mentioned my own. Was he that much tougher than me? Was I too sensitive? I could never frame the right questions to probe what was going on with my brother.

◆ ◆ ◆

For weeks after that dinner party, my *Rolling Stone* colleagues drooled every time I said that Jayne was in town and would be cooking that night, stirring thoughts of sitting at our counter in Chelsea with a Tex-Mex plate sprinkled with tender and pungent spices.

How sad we all were when Jayne moved to Arlington, Virginia to work on a film. Although she kept the keys to the walkup and stayed there when in New York, she transported her belongings and most of her spirit south. My annual *Rolling Stone* salary, upped to ten thousand dollars, could accommodate living without a roommate. I spread out into the large bedroom, turning the other room into my study.

The urge to write tugged at me, especially as I ran to the city's tip and took in the enormity of Manhattan's tallest towers shadowing land sheared off into dark water. My mother would give Robert and me sheets of lined paper in the evenings after dinner, after homework was done. "Write," she would say. "I don't care what you write. Just write." I'd chew on the pencil nub and let thoughts flow into my head, then quickly dash the image into words. Robert's perfect sentences, lyrical, often depicted changing seasons. Mine were more escapist—a fallen tree transformed into a canoe rushing down a river or a bicycle ride down unexplored roads into a different world. That nightly drill carried me through college, my mother's coxswain voice, *just write*, urging me to the end of many bluebook exams.

Being a writer took courage. I would have to live, really *live*, fight for what I believed, like Karen Silkwood had. There would be rejection, repeatedly. I would have to instill discipline to keep going. *Just write.* I silently vowed to do so as I jogged home.

On the Lower East Side, I found a cherry wood secretary desk with a base of wide drawers topped by a hinged writing surface. Bookshelves above the desk elegantly closed with a pair of cut-glass doors. A tall and heavy piece of furniture, I paid dearly to have it moved, to become my centerpiece item holding cherished books and my Olivetti typewriter. I sat there in the evenings to *just write*, giving lives to nameless people. I was working on a short story about three women and the question as to whether they were really one person. I managed to concentrate. Yet when the phone rang, there was always the hope of someone asking to meet up at a bar or nightclub.

Most of what I wrote at *Rolling Stone* was rejection letters, the very things I most feared. A stack of envelopes falling on my desk each morning formed the slush pile, requiring only a quick enough perusal to ensure it didn't contain the next Hunter Thompson or Tom Wolfe. Occasionally I might find something to pass on to Paul. More often than not the pages would be given back to me for the perfunctory, but nonetheless cruel, rejection.

I thought about the people at the other end of my rejections when I sat in my study and could not type. They wrote and sent out what they wrote; I dawdled. Tables turned, I could be the rejected one. But not forever, not if I wrote every day, developed my voice, found the right outlets for my work, and tried harder to get more on the pages of *Rolling Stone*.

I gave up cigarettes and ran twenty to thirty miles a week, but what was I running from or to? Finally some direction came from Gloria Emerson, who joined the *Rolling Stone* crew as News & Opinions editor. Older, a veteran of Vietnam as correspondent for the *New York Times*, she came by my desk in her tall patrician manner, cigarette holder between her fingers, waving a clip about women being allowed to join the US Marines.

"You're a young healthy woman. Join up and write an exposé for the magazine."

I laughed.

Gloria persisted. "Don't you want to be a Marine?"

Emphatic "No."

"Why not?"

I described sitting in front of the television with my brother during the draft lottery. "He didn't want to be drafted into service and possibly sent to Vietnam. Why would I voluntarily join?"

"Well, then," she said, starting to turn away. Then she stopped, and just glared at me. "Going to Vietnam opened my eyes to many things. At some point, if you want to be a writer, you're going to have to take the plunge into things that you dread."

I knew she was right. I would never be a writer until I ventured dangerously far outside my comfort zone. Just not to a barracks on a military base. Not then.

CHAPTER 9

Leaving my comfort zone would ultimately involve a far more painful initiation than might have occurred on a Marine base. I would have to rifle through long-gone years in search of clues I had missed. And I would have to ask myself, again and again—*What could I have done differently?*

My brother mostly treaded in silent manipulative mystery. Yet some of his actions did reveal a glimpse into the caverns of his damaged mind. I just didn't know what I could do, as the oft-disregarded little sister, to make him better, even when he cried out in 1977.

"Robert is in the hospital." My mother's voice on the phone, trembling.

I clutched the phone cord and collapsed on the sofa. "What happened?"

"He swallowed a bottle of aspirin. They just pumped out his stomach."

"Is he okay?"

"He will be. He did something awful. I'm ashamed for him," she said, "and for me."

What could be so terrible, and did any of it matter if Robert was all right?

My mother kept talking. "Turns out he's been stealing shirts from Apollo and selling them on the side."

"Why would he do that?"

"I don't know Susan. I really don't know. Morty caught him and sent him home. That's where he swallowed the aspirin. Harold found him and got him to the hospital."

I thought immediately of my father and how the family had treated him after his crimes. Would they shun Robert now too? Call him a monster? Make him go far away?

"Did Uncle Morty fire Robert?"

"No, of course not. He's worried, like we're all worried. This isn't like Robbie. My son is better than this."

I knew how good Robert was; I also knew the master manipulator, knew him far better than my mother did. When we were younger I watched him trick people, simple things like selling his friends "special" rubber bands that could be used to ping unsuspecting victims. His orthodontist handed the tiny bands out in bulk after filling his mouth with metal braces. Robert traded those tiny weapons for nickels and dimes. The older he got, the more he could wield the power of his personality. He could be everyone's best friend and say exactly what they wanted to hear. He appeared unflappable and in charge. But I saw his tricks, the way he could flash on and off, charming, then not. I just didn't know what all this meant. As I spoke to my mother, though, all I could think about was my brother's pain. Something had broken down in the vulnerable scheme of his life, and he was most likely as confounded as we were.

"Will he be in the hospital long?"

"They're evaluating him now." I could hear exhaustion in her voice.

"Should I come home?"

"No." She was adamant. "It's better you stay in New York. He's feeling very self-conscious about letting everyone down. The fewer people he sees right now the better. He'll get his strength back."

He had to—he was my rock. Who else could I call in the middle of the night when in despair? Horribly worried for him, I could make no sense of what he had done. He didn't need the money he got from selling those purloined shirts. His petty thievery was an obvious cry for help, but everyone around him, everyone who loved him—including me—only wanted to see this incident as a blip. None of us looked further than his recovery, anxious to see him back on his feet. We all skated over what had made him commit those uncharacteristic acts.

"This too shall pass." My mother's favorite mantra. But some things would not pass, would linger, like the hollow forming in my chest that even New York City could not fill.

Robert had given me a sewing machine when I graduated college. After I got off the phone, I removed the Olivetti typewriter from my desk and replaced it with his gift. If my mother did not want me to see Robert, I would sew my brother a beautiful quilt that could embrace him like my arms very much wanted to do. I spent an entire Saturday morning combing through the fashion district off Seventh Avenue for fabric stores that would sell me odds and ends. I bought a yard of very soft brown material used for polishing metals, something to bring back the shine of his smile. From a different merchant, I chose a remnant of blue-and-white embossed cotton that made me think of high clouds on a summer sky, reminiscent of the sweetness of his favorite season. I chose some bold colors too, for fortitude through his recovery.

Creating patterns of geometric shapes, I cut the fabrics into many interconnecting pieces. Yet I could never capture Robert's complexity. He had changed after high school, especially after flunking out of Penn State. Such a cavalier manner he assumed immediately afterward toward everyone, especially me. Something was going on inside his head, but nothing I could penetrate. Even his room in that small apartment was locked with him isolated inside. He would lift weights and play music, mostly the Doors with Jim Morrison's mystical voice lamenting what happens when you're strange. Robert did come out of that funk and once again put on a perfect smile and rejoined those who regaled Big K. He again ran with his pack in College Park. Far away at college in Wisconsin, I could only hope my brother was flourishing in his comfortable milieu. We spoke sporadically; him, often too busy to say much more than "Hey sis doing great, hope you are too." Back then he proved to be an acrobat, elastically upright after a precarious roll. In actuality, though, he was a wrestler, and wrestlers do sometimes get pinned to the mat. I did not know if he would easily recover from this takedown.

I worked on that sewing machine over several weeks, finally producing a small but colorful quilt that I sent to Robert. I had emptied myself—my emotions, my love—into cobbling together those many varied shapes. I had poured my pain over Robert's self-destructive action into something tightly constructed. It would have to hold up.

Wanting to do more for my brother, I could only think to ease his pain in a way that would have eased mine. I asked chief music critic Dave Marsh if, perhaps, he would let Robert try his hand at a record review. Robert had been the first to suggest in the late 1960s that a group of us go to the Merriweather Post Pavilion in Columbia, Maryland, to hear the Who do their rock opera about a deaf, dumb, and blind boy named Tommy. He made his friend Brian take me along as his date. One of the best-looking upperclassmen in high school, I was delighted to go with Brian but was not sure about the music. A rock opera? But I trusted Robert. I would not have had a social life without being his little sister. Being able to experience the Who's *Tommy* that night on Robert's recommendation is something I will never forget.

I knocked on Dave's door, a tad nervous.

When Jayne had come by with a request to write reviews, Dave told her bluntly that he would give her an album to review if one came in produced by a woman. In a music recording industry sewn up by men, little likelihood of that existed in 1977.

Dave looked up and saw me standing there. "Hi, Susan. Something you need?"

"Yes."

He beckoned me inside his office. I explained that my brother had hit a bad stretch working in my uncle's shirt factory in Baltimore and clearly needed a fresh start. "Would you give Robert a chance at writing record reviews?"

Dave let his brown cigarette fall into a half-filled beer bottle and pulled out a sheet of masthead stationary. He wrote down a phone number. "You tell Robert to call me. It's my home number. I'll walk him through the drill and then send him some albums."

Robert never called Dave despite my imploring him to. Writing for *Rolling Stone* was my idea, not his. Robert told me that he was too busy—a lie, one I could see straight through. I thought about how much he said that I could not penetrate. Stabbing thoughts rattled me for days. Robert had drifted far beyond my reach. He was back working at the Apollo shirt factory and pretending that everything was all right.

◆   ◆   ◆

My father, often doing business with banks in New York City, wanted to have dinner. I was hoping he might have ideas for getting Robert on more solid footing. Since Dad kept bankers' hours for his real estate transactions, he would be finished at 4 p.m., chatting up everyone at the bar until I arrived. By the time I showed up he had drunk down several beers and knew everyone sitting near him by first name. "Here's my daughter," he exclaimed when I walked into Trader Vic's, a Polynesian restaurant in the Plaza Hotel.

"Look at her. Just a baby such a short time ago, and now she's working at the *Rolling Stone*." He turned to the man next to him at the bar. "You ever hear of Rolling Stones? I hadn't, but now I know that it's the real deal. She's got herself a real magazine job."

I managed to extricate him from the bar area and get the hostess to put us at a table far in the back beside the fake waterfall. As much as he had embarrassed me, I also liked his show of pride. Praise had always been saved for the high-achieving Robert.

When the waitress came over, I held on tight to the cocktail menu. "That's all Dad. I'm cutting you off."

"But I was just starting to feel good," he told me. "And you haven't asked, but I had a very successful day at the banks."

No matter how many times I mentioned Robert, my father skirted the very painful subject of his son's breakdown.

"I'm worried," he said. "Andy is getting to be an old dog." My Dad talked about that large, shaggy poodle through dinner like a player needle stuck in a record groove.

Looking at him in the finely tailored suit that managed to streamline his large frame and his white hair cut to minimize the cowlicks, my father was presentable. The Navy officer who had married my mother was dashing, slender, could even pull off carrying a pipe occasionally. Yet he had gone through the wringer after disbarment and divorce. Some of my earliest memories are of him running that fleabag motel, when his clothes did not fit so well, and his dark hair was filled with gray. Those were his Vagabond years, and ours. It was not until we were teenagers that Robert admitted how much he had hated going to the Vagabond. I only recalled all the adventures we had shared. Shirley's two children, Barbara and Steve, both a decade older than Robert and me, despised having had to experience some of their high school years in Aberdeen and in such a motel as the Vagabond. That motel has remained an embarrassment to everyone in the family but me, so mesmerized by what might have gone on in those rooms that even now I sometimes think of the odd allure of those cheap curtains and flickering gaslights.

The turning point in my father's life is a story he repeated often: Borrowing money, acquiring land, landing K-Mart and the A&P as anchor stores. He had nearly completed the Summerdale Plaza on the south side of the Susquehanna River in Harrisburg in the mid-1960s. All he needed was another million dollars to make it real. Unfortunately, US banks turned off the tap. He went to a wealthy businessman with a seasoned reputation and offered to sell him the entire project for that final installment. The man said no.

Dad continued the story after he had ordered battered shrimp and a platter of other appetizers to soak up the beer. "That man could have had it all. Summerdale would be his now instead of mine. But he refused. And did I give up?"

I could finish the story for him. No, he did not give up. Dad went to a bank in Germany and borrowed the money. After Summerdale was completed, he leveraged equity from the booming strip mall and bought more land and built more and more.

"Robert needs a different job," I blurted.

"I'm working on it. But Andy, he can't even get in the car anymore without my help."

Dad slipped me a month's rent as we parted, smiling through the pain that suddenly clouded his eyes, and told me, "Just stay as happy as you are right now."

CHAPTER 10

"Where's the Toad?"

I never heard Gloria Emerson refer to *Rolling Stone* editor and publisher Jann Wenner as anything but a squat amphibian with warts. If Jann ever heard the unflattering moniker, I'm certain he laughed.

"What rock has he hopped under now? Tell me, I know he's hiding somewhere."

Gloria could never slip into a room. Not simply her towering six-foot height, not just that the former war correspondent blurted anything on her mind, but because she refused to be ignored.

Talking at a fast clip, she went on, "I told him to stay away from my writers. And what does the Toad do? I'll tell you what. He takes poor Michael Herr into his office and sends him out so confused he doesn't know where he is."

In his quest to conquer New York, Jann had courted Gloria after she published her National Book Award-winning *Winners and Losers*. Although it had nothing to do with rock and roll, her dramatic prose exposed raw emotions in people torn by war, much as the magazine sought to do in its long feature stories that wrung out the underside of contemporary culture. She agreed to edit the magazine's News & Opinion section on the premise that she might bring serious politics and writers to a publication she had rarely read and often dismissed. Once situated in the *Rolling Stone* newsroom, Gloria became the eccentric aunt in a den of untamable ruffians.

Gloria and Michael were part of a journalism cadre recently returned from Vietnam with enough literary muscle to forever change the way correspondents cover war, their words and images so penetratingly sharp as to slice away the distance between reader and battle. While Gloria's book explored the psychological damage inflicted on both sides from the war, Michael's *Dispatches* offered graphically vivid insights on war, battle, and the human condition.

The befuddled, soft-spoken man who had just walked out of *Rolling Stone*'s offices bore little resemblance to the brittle edgy narrator of *Dispatches*, the memoir that John Le Carré had declared "the best book I have ever read on men and war in our time." Michael had smiled somewhat vacantly as he prepared to leave, tucked his papers under his arm and then forgot they were there when he reached out to shake my hand. I helped him gather his things and he thanked me profusely.

When Gloria couldn't find Jann, she pulled me into her office. "I told the Toad not to give Michael anything." She paced, lit a menthol cigarette, bunched her dark pageboy hair with fidgety fingers.

I tried to calm her. "Maybe Jann gave him an assignment to get him back to writing."

"Oh Pony, you're so naïve. Michael needs much more than an assignment to write."

I was Pony. Said with considerable affection, Gloria saw me as one of those Budweiser Clydesdales that pull heavy loads. Nearly twice my age, she grew to rely on me as someone who wouldn't falter, no matter how difficult the tasks. She had apparently forgotten I would not join the Marines to do an exposé as one of the first females to enlist. In fact, Gloria decided to mold me into a journalist. I did not know if I had the gumption to be a real reporter firing tough questions at powerful people. I always thought of myself as a fiction writer. I was in a program in college that guided me in that direction, and I'd written many short stories. But I wanted adventure, and this woman appeared ready to take me on one.

Robert had always been the adventurous instigator, yanking his kid sister along on road trips that once landed me at a weekend music festival with four boys and a Sunday visit to a local judge's house to pay a speeding ticket as we raced home on back-country Pennsylvania roads. How excited I was to be included on this excursion to hear some very good local bands. I never expected to spend the night outside under the stars as the music kept going and going. We had hardly anything to eat, but enough wine to make me nearly forget the hunger. At some point in the early dawn, a plane flying low overhead dropped parcels of ice cream and we all lunged for the cardboard cartons. When we could finally return to the car, everyone clamored that they had to get home. Fast. When the cop pulled us over, Robert tried to talk him out of writing a ticket, pointing to me—squeezed in the backseat between teenage boys—and saying how urgently I had to be somewhere. Even at the peak of his powers, though, Robert failed to convince the cop not to issue the ticket.

That cunning Robert had returned, at least in my mind; him, ever jolly again, feigning he had never buckled under. Swallowing the aspirin was just a slip up, he had implied when we last spoke, and I let it go. I so desperately wanted to believe him. Just as I had wanted to believe years earlier that a car trip to a music festival would not get rowdy and cost us plenty to pay off the judge.

As Gloria's career path had been tough, she had no intention of making it smoother for me. She simply wanted me to understand how to do the reporter's job right: her way. I loved being the recipient of her attention and happily did as she asked. No one had ever taken such interest in me. Under her tutelage, I began to believe I could become a journalist.

Still fuming over the Toad's cornering of Michael Herr, Gloria decided later that day that we should leave the office. This would be a "burger night," not dinner. She remained pointedly firm about the distinction—one being a working meal, the other, a social occasion. We grabbed the Fifth Avenue bus toward Washington Square Park and jumped off before Fourteenth Street.

"What was the woman sitting next to you wearing?" she asked immediately after the bus doors shut.

"Red?" I had hardly noticed the woman on the bus.

"She wore orange stripes. Details, details, details, Pony. You must absorb everything around you and take careful mental notes. Who was this person sitting beside you? Does she have a story?"

"She never said anything." My defense fell as flat as the asphalt avenue we were crossing to the tavern.

Gloria leaned half a foot down to my level. "You have to search to find the story. Look for a wedding ring, what book she's reading, the quality of her shoes."

She abruptly changed the subject to ask about my "assignment." She had wanted me to write something, on any subject, and I chose an angle on the Karen Silkwood case that Howard Kohn had not covered: why Silkwood ignited such a broad following of activists from labor to feminists. Howard's meticulous accounts of her suspicious death continued to haunt me (as Howard began to obsess me). Some supporters thought Karen had been intentionally pushed off the road on her way to meet the *New York Times* reporter with incriminating evidence against her employer, Kerr-McGee. Naysayers said she crashed because of her own recklessness and drug use. The legal case that Silkwood's family brought against the nuclear firm involved safety violations in the workplace. Lawyers alleged that Karen, a lab technician, had been contaminated by plutonium. Howard was investigating whether Kerr-McGee had, in fact, retaliated against Karen for exposing radioactive dangers. My article delved into the capricious woman who, in death, reemerged as a mighty focal point.

I did not admit to Gloria how much Karen's story inspired me. Like Joan of Arc, Karen would not capitulate when they tormented her by planting plutonium-tainted bologna in her refrigerator and much worse. I, too, wanted to believe in something so strongly that I would walk through fire. I just didn't know yet what would spur the fighter in me.

Once inside the tavern, we found every table occupied. I thought we would go somewhere else, but Gloria stood her ground. "Okay Pony, now I'll show you how to push out tiresome people who won't leave."

Gloria leaned like a flamingo over a booth with two lingering diners. Her long neck extended, one leg jutting forward, her eyes cast down at coffee mugs that remained on the nearly cleared table. Then she fixated on their faces with a bird-beak stare, her eyes round behind black-rimmed glasses.

I could not hear what the couple said, but they managed to squeeze past Gloria in their quick exodus from the table. Gloria sat down before busboys could clear the debris. She pushed away the menus and ordered for us—burgers, fries, and beer on tap.

I told her that *Seven Days* magazine had expressed some interest in publishing my Silkwood article.

"Now that's a magazine trying desperately to define the remnants of liberalism."

"I interned there. They offered me a job—"

"It's where you should be, Pony. *Rolling Stone* is for music kooks. Not you. You should offer up your energies to make the world better."

Perhaps, but I was not ready to leave *Rolling Stone*, especially not when an award-winning author was showing such interest in me.

"Your writers aren't music kooks," I argued. "Certainly not Lally Weymouth."

Daughter of *Washington Post* publisher Katherine Graham, Lally had just finished a feature story on fashion goddess Diana Vreeland under the tutelage of Gloria. I helped them get the finished product to San Francisco on deadline. Using clear tape, Gloria had rearranged the story scribbled throughout with her bold editing in black ink. My job was to quickly proof and then slip the tape-slapped pages through the Mojo machine's slender opening and telefax it to the copyeditors. "A real cut-and-paste job," I had joked because the cliché seemed funny at the moment.

"Yes," Gloria repeated at the purloined table after the burgers were served. "You would be a much better fit at *Seven Days.*"

Working with Gloria, writing about Karen Silkwood, made me long for some real action. My antiwar activities had taken place in the waning days of the struggle, days already tainted with nostalgia for the real protests of the late sixties. In the early seventies, Watergate events followed by Nixon's fall were more machinations of the establishment than upheaval by the people. And then the late seventies settled in, after the hoopla, like a dry alcoholic.

Jimmy Carter's Washington offered a Southern gentility that slipped white gloves on uplifted fists. I spent a night in Washington visiting friends. Everything was so new and elegant, the city and its buildings endlessly white. Race riots and war protests were a distant echo.

Even back in New York, working at what was considered a counterculture publication, I could not quite shake the sense of sloshing through lukewarm waters. A foot soldier in getting out a publication every two weeks was hardly leading a charge.

CHAPTER 11

Howard Kohn would satisfy in me the political fervor that Gloria had only awakened. When Howard pointed me toward a vibrant grassroots movement emerging around nuclear power plants, I saw a battle taking shape where my ability to do something might matter. Something about him had captivated me even before we met in person. His ongoing series on the Karen Silkwood case had everything—heroism, possible murder, workplace harassment, and dangerous flaws in the nuclear industry. Howard's mysterious past also held an allure. As a young award-winning reporter for the *Detroit Free Press*, Howard had staked out a very dangerous story covering the heroin trade in that city. People were already in jail because of his reporting, and Howard was getting ever closer to nailing the kingpins when he was arrested for giving a false account of an attempt on his life. Fired from his job and rebuilding his life in

San Francisco, Jann Wenner made the smart decision to give this star reporter another chance. In all the years that I have known Howard, I never asked him why he claimed to have been kidnapped and held at gunpoint. What broke him down? Not long after I arrived, the magazine published Howard's feature story on his father's dairy farm that somewhat explained his cow-wrangling instincts. When he circled a story, he didn't stop until he had roped his sources. I knew Howard was married. His wife, Diana, was Jann's assistant in San Francisco. Choosing not to move to New York City with the rest of the entourage, Howard and Diana would help anchor a San Francisco annex.

My early fascination with Howard, akin to a schoolgirl crush, had another side. I respected Gloria, but I wanted *to be* Howard. He could shake up the world with his investigative journalism. And he performed this feat with a mild manner that disarmed sources and a fierce writing style that nailed the details. Gloria knew how to get inside people. Howard could penetrate dangerous networks and, as I pictured it, pore through classified documents in unlit cubicles. Dogged. Relentless.

At Howard's suggestion, I closely followed the environmental movement just beginning to protest the invisible dangers of nuclear power plants. These activists were back-to-the-land types who wanted the simplicity of clean living and were savvy enough to sense that the energy conglomerates investing in nuclear power were blowing poisons in the wind. I was always cutting out articles on this growing movement and sending them to Howard via interoffice mail.

Then I received a note back on which he scrawled, "Let me take you to dinner next week when I'm in New York. It will be a way to thank you for all your help." I reread it several times. My fingers studied his words as my fast-beating heart rushed blood to my head. My imagination already had us together, me being touched with hands calloused from years on the dairy farm. My face beet red, I escaped to the restroom until I could pull myself together. I took his note with me, ran a fingertip along the curls of his letters, tried to think what type of pen he used. I didn't know him hardly at all, but I knew I would fall in love.

Our dinner stretched into a weekend.

There are many moments of those first days together forever etched in my memories, more as sensations, stomach-lunging excitement, walking for miles and not noticing the tread of the sidewalk for the arm encircling my shoulder, or the way spiced food tasted with its savory glaze when sliding into my mouth from his fork.

Some of the details are jotted in my journal:

Long walks through Chinatown, the Staten Island Ferry in the wee hours of the morning, clutching in the movie theater, the Chelsea Hotel, baseball in the park, last-minute talks before a plane departure.

At the end of our first evening, Howard followed me up those five flights and into my apartment as if I were leading him home. The dim lights of New York City seemed to concentrate on us as we burrowed into the contours of each other's bodies. Never before had Patti Smith's words had such resonance. That night, with Howard's legs entwined with mine, belonged to lovers.

I felt intensely desired. Everything about him thrilled me. His green eyes, light fine hair, slender, but mostly it was his smile that appealed to me, almost like a signal that all was right with the world. The way he dressed, in inexpensive synthetics that he threw on as a second thought, always the country boy. Mostly I was drawn in by something in his manner, his ability to appear much meeker and less sharp than he actually was. His soft gaze on me the first time we met, and his continued attention, never too conspicuous so that others might notice.

Howard talked during our twenty-five-cent ride on the Staten Island ferry, with the approaching Statue of Liberty vivid in the moonlight, of turning the Karen Silkwood story into a film starring Talia Shire. This was a far cry from Meryl Streep, who would portray Karen in the 1983 movie based on the book that Howard eventually wrote, *Who Killed Karen Silkwood?* A dark-eyed waif-like Karen, Talia had winningly played Connie Corleone in the Godfather movies. That this portrayal of a bruised wife of mafia violence had somehow captured Howard's heart intrigued me. Where did I fit in between his wife and these other women? I never let myself dwell on that too long.

After Howard returned to San Francisco, we exchanged handwritten notes through the interoffice mail with increasing intensity. Each afternoon I waited for a missive from Howard, disappointed if nothing came in the daily pouch. I sent him a clip from the *Village Voice* on the banning of antinuclear films. How careful I was not to reveal to those around me the flush in my cheeks as I jotted innocuous words on a slip of paper. Howard responded in a similar tone to my note—innuendoes, casual, wondering who might be looking over his shoulder, I imagined. He spoke of the "nuke" industry fighting to the end and that he would play at our *Rolling Stone* softball game in late July. He took such pride in being on the magazine's softball team. I had no choice but to bide my time until I could be with him again.

At the Strand bookstore one evening I found a mention of Howard in a book that had come out the year before, in 1976— *The Investigative Journalist: Folk Heroes of a New Era* by James H. Dygert—and bought it as a gift for Robert. Howard's work with David Weir on the Patty Hearst story got a few lines, enough to pump up my heart rate. While other reporters were attending press briefings, Howard and David retraced Patty's steps and exposed where she had been during her two years on the run. I thought the book might inspire Robert, and bought it for him, but these chapters on investigative reporters only inspired me. My brother laughed and suggested I keep the book.

I was projecting my fanciful, delusionary self on Robert. Like Don Quixote of the post-Watergate era, I would ride my steed with pen in hand into any battle. Why couldn't Robert share my fervent desire to right all the wrongs? How little I understood my brother, to have assumed he would share my political fight. My brother was steeped in an altogether different struggle, restraining mounds of buried pain. The suddenness of Dad's departure, and then his being openly vilified, must have pummeled Robert's sense of his very young self. My brother reacted by inflating his own personality, becoming the remarkable person everyone had to adore. How difficult it must have been for him to contain that bruised child, keep that part of his psyche hidden for all those years.

I was the luckier one. Much of my childhood was spent spinning elaborate fantasies that removed me from bitter family dynamics. This wild imagination of my younger years became more sophisticated as I reached my twenties and greatly magnified the excitement of being at *Rolling Stone*, having affairs, working with rock stars on No Nukes. I may have been running on exploding passions and heading for a crash landing but nothing lay festering inside me.

CHAPTER 12

Gloria looked out over Central Park from large windows in her freshly painted office in the new *Rolling Stone* headquarters at 745 Fifth Avenue. Rather than appear pleased with her new view, Gloria grimaced. "This is it, Pony." She spread her arms wide, taking in the full panorama twenty-three floors below: primped greenery spread out for miles, the Plaza Hotel, horse-drawn carriages, Bergdorf Goodman, people scurrying with packages into limousines and taxis.

"It doesn't get any crasser," she announced.

Moving a cultural icon from San Francisco to New York City proved as transformative to the magazine as a sex-change operation. *Rolling Stone* lost its in-your-face cocky demeanor when the West Coast contingent got stripped down, packed up, and shipped cross-country in a brigade of slow-moving vans.

In these lavish new offices, fresh fruit juice dispensers were installed in the production area to give the Californians the semblance of natural sunshine in the grit of Manhattan. Whether the pulpy orange juice appeased their craving for home, I could never determine. When I gave a visiting Hunter Thompson a tour of the new digs, he expressed his enthusiasm for the dispenser by shaking the machine and yelling, "Mixers!" The Gonzo journalist often showed up in New York when he was close to deadline on a big piece, allowing editors to keep a close eye on this notable procrastinator. On one visit, Iris gave me an envelope filled with cash to take across the street to the Plaza Hotel—as it turned out, a required deposit since Hunter had taken his gun and shot out all the light fixtures in the hotel room during his prior stay.

Being folded into these new headquarters for *Rolling Stone,* with my newsroom desk situated outside Gloria's office and very much in the hubbub of activity, thrilled me. Burger night tutorials continued with the tall older woman leading me down Fifth Avenue on foot rather than running to catch buses. Gloria loved traipsing past all the huge department stores with changing fashion art windows. She once pulled me inside Bergdorf Goodman to show me the designer section. Gloria's clothes were always impeccable: tightly belted skirts and silk blouses that hung coolly even in the summer heat. Running her hands across a rack of Dior, she said in her pitched enunciation, "Do you know what this is Pony? This is fine fabric, finely designed. Know it, but never let it turn you into a materialistic person." She swiftly pirouetted from the designers. "You shouldn't come in here again. You can't afford these clothes and you shouldn't make it a goal to own such things. You're better than this." With that, we left Bergdorf's.

Pausing to light a menthol cigarette, Gloria asked, "Did I tell you that the Toad wants to kill the interview with La Pasionaria? He says his magazine readers don't care about the Spanish Civil War since it's *ancient* history. Can you believe that, Pony?"

"How horrible. Merle worked so hard on that piece." I often befriended freelance journalists, envying their bravery at being out there writing and hawking articles.

"Remind me to request a kill fee for Merle tomorrow."

Poor Merle, who called every day to see when the lengthy interview she had conducted in Spanish (and then translated) with the woman who fought Fascism would run in *Rolling Stone* magazine.

I absorbed Gloria's indignation for Jann's killing of this article, an interview with a true heroine, Dolores Ibárruri, battle name La Pasionaria, or Passion Flower. She was imprisoned many times, battle weary, separated from family. What does it take to have that kind of courage? I imagined it took a cause worth dying for. What might such a crusading cause be for me?

The next time we went out, Gloria carried a stack of "Boycott J. P. Stevens" leaflets. Organized labor was targeting the Southern textile company for being so aggressively nonunion. Go into the linen departments of all the department stores and leave the leaflets right on the stacks of colorful sheets and towels manufactured by the union-busting villains, Gloria instructed.

I loved it, brushing past New York shoppers and scattering leaflets among the rows of bed and bathroom fabrics. My energy charged as I walked into those massive rooms hung with intimate drapery made for empresses. I imagined myself branding this evil product. *J. P. Stevens is unfair to workers.* Anyone who rolled in these sheets would be a traitor to American labor. Two years later, in 1979, Sally Field as Norma Rae drove home the need for unionization of the textile industry far more dramatically than I could. But I was out there ahead of the movie, wearing *Boycott J. P. Stevens* buttons and depositing leaflets demanding justice. Had anyone tried to forcibly remove me, I would have stood on the highest table and screamed, "Power to the workers."

Becoming a journalist wasn't all frolic, Gloria reminded me. Our lessons merely spun the thread for constructing articles. But I was left fumbling with how to stitch a narrative voice.

Rolling Stone did not provide an opportunity for me to write much more than headlines and rejection letters. I had to practice Gloria's teachings on my Olivetti. Often when I tried to write at home my thoughts went elsewhere. I couldn't get Howard out of my mind. He had not returned to New York since our romantic weekend. When I typed, I saw his smile, maroon coat, tie, and polyester black pants. No matter how aware I was of the impossibility of our ever being a real couple, I very much enjoyed the fantasy.

From the opposite coast, I followed Howard as he wrote long feature pieces on everything from the CIA and the Burger Court to follow-ups on the Silkwood story, offering what assistance I could from New York. I still wondered whether I wanted him or wanted to be him, a multifaceted writer with the ability to stab at America's power matrix.

It was Gloria, though, who worked with me on putting together sentences that articulated themes of societal inequities. She made me concentrate on digging up details that supported what I wrote. But sitting down at the typewriter often seemed laborious compared to being outside with leaflets or involved in other forms of protest.

When longtime peace activist and social justice leader Cora Weiss organized a celebration of post-war Vietnam's admission to the United Nations, Gloria suggested that Cora call me. In no time, Cora had me selling tickets to the Riverside Church event that, among other things, would honor North Vietnamese dignitaries. I convinced many people in the newsroom to buy tickets, insisting that UN acceptance was an important stage for peace and healing.

Flippant staffers like Chuck Young and Dave Marsh taunted me, much as Robert had when we were young. My brother knew exactly how to puncture my enthusiasm with a single line.

"You have no friends," Robert once fired, after I'd called him "Roberta" for wrapping a towel around his torso. His words hurt because they were true.

He also knew how to grill my intelligence. "I bet you don't know who the current vice president is," he'd shout.

When I fumbled, as I invariably would, he would smack the table and declare, "Hubert Humphrey."

Robert often belittled me during those tension-filled years in our small apartment. He knew my every vulnerability. By ribbing me until I was close to tears, he could feel mighty. At school, or out with his friends, he was Big K strutting his stuff. At home, though, the cramped space cornered him, and he lashed out.

Chuck and Dave irritated me, but they could never get under my skin, as Robert had.

"We fought the North Vietnamese and lost. Why should we honor the commies now?" Dave asked.

I argued that the unified country needed to rebuild and that the basic human rights of its entire people had to be respected.

Chuck, sneering, declared, "The Socialist Republic of Vietnam are murderers."

Angered, I lost my ability to form a rational response. Instead, I spewed words about a healing nation until Chuck paid for a ticket simply to shut me up.

"You have the right instincts," Gloria told me afterward, "but you have to shape more compelling arguments that grab people and make them as angry as you are."

I was angry, and I didn't even know why. Was it political? Personal?

The Baltimore where I grew up was a city of sharp contrasts, not just Black and White or Greek/Italian/Irish immigrants pocketed in isolated neighborhoods, but Russian Jews eschewed by German Jews and the upwardly mobile towering over the stuck. Although ensconced in a low-rent apartment complex, I had constant exposure to the country club world of affluent suburban Jews through my mother's better-married sisters. Their wealth had pomposity: big *macher* at the synagogue, home in Barbados, and multiple foreign cars that didn't have rusted craters in the back, as did our Floorless Flyer.

Not entirely ungrateful, I did enjoy splashing in a cold pool during hot Baltimore summers as a guest at my aunts' fancy Jewish country clubs. I especially liked going to my Aunt Naomi's house outside Washington. In her backyard was an Olympic-sized swimming pool, tennis courts, and a large patio where she served cold gazpacho in round mugs for lunch and cool drinks throughout the day. But I was invisible. There but not noticed. Just a slip of a girl lost in a billowy bathing suit, going off the diving board over and over again. Most likely, I was imagining myself as a competitor, every leap or dive off that board being wildly cheered by imaginary voices in my head.

Summer family days were different for Robert. He would sit by the pool with his perfectly tanned and muscled physique and awe everyone with his charm and humor. "They threw away the mold after they made Robert," Aunt Shifra once told my mother.

Gloria's efforts to expose me to the dangers of wealth merely recalled being that unnoticed relative, something rooted inside me like venom. My mother's sisters had driven in the wedge that split apart my parents' marriage. Mom could have stood by the man she had married. Instead, her siblings brushed my father off like dirty lint after his crimes surfaced, told him to his face he was worth far less than his life insurance. And my mother listened. I like to believe that she had her doubts about whether to throw him out of the house. She must have considered, even briefly, how devastating losing a father in those circumstances would be for Robert and me. She must have recalled that she once loved this man she had married.

My parents were happy together, back in the early years after the war when Dad zipped through law school at the University of Virginia. My mother often spoke of the tiny house on Ivy Street they had bought in Charlottesville, a few rooms with a tin roof and plywood floors that she lovingly furnished around a single kerosene heater. She talked of friends gathering on the spur of the moment to play bridge in their pajamas—friends who I would later meet, who always spoke very fondly of my dad. My mother never stopped smiling when reminiscing about Charlottesville. Yet she let that world go.

No one told us what had happened for a very long time. We only knew Dad did something horrible. Like a Greek tragedy, the father's crimes—magnified and dramatized by a family chorus—would imprint on the children, destined to experience their own calamities.

I slowly understood that having your family name on a synagogue auditorium does not make one a good person. Showy foreign cars attract younger women and infidelity. So much hypocrisy was etched on this rich family around us. Becoming a journalist and exposing inequalities became the obvious direction I could take to finally discharge my inner rebelliousness. But that would have to wait.

CHAPTER 13

On the day we lost Elvis Presley in August of 1977, I had to consider—even just for a moment—that the king of rock and roll had collapsed off the toilet while attempting to take a shit. The official cause of death was cardiac arrhythmia. In truth, he'd had a cocktail of prescribed drugs that included morphine, Demerol, Valium, Codeine, and Quaaludes.

As everyone in the newsroom huddled to discuss what would be written, and by whom, all I could see was Elvis' oiled hair in the '61 film *Blue Hawaii* during my eighth birthday party when his swaying hips did nothing more than make me quietly laugh into my hands. I had been mortified only an hour earlier when my father came to pick us up for ice cream and the movies. None of my friends knew what divorce even was until the moment that my father knocked on our door with his car motor still running. My fabricated stories of a normal family life were flagrantly exposed.

With trepidation, I had walked into the bathroom the night before as my mother lay in the tub relaxing and finally admitted that I had been lying to my friends. I pleaded with her to help me out by allowing my father in the house before my friends arrived. She flatly refused, gave me a lecture on lying, and allowed my father's awkward arrival to raise the dreaded question.

"He doesn't live here?" a young friend asked, eyes like dartboards.

"No dear," my mother answered. "Susie's father and I are divorced." She said it so matter-of-fact.

Forever after, Elvis's music recalled for me that horrible moment of humiliation. I had been found out as a blatant liar—worse, as a kid different from the others, with parents split apart like chicken splayed for the fryer. As Elvis fought so hard to be provocative, his swaying hips on the big screen should have shown me that being different can be bold. But at age eight, I couldn't see the bigger picture.

Elvis' death proved untimely in many ways. His too-young demise happened to fall on the eve of *Rolling Stone*'s first issue to be produced in New York and, as planned for months, contained many pieces celebrating the city. So those famous hips and rhythmic swing killed the Bella Abzug/Andy Warhol cover as surely as they had killed Elvis. Instead of New York's famously hatted Bella, who would appear in the following issue, the king of rock and roll would be forever memorialized on the *Rolling Stone* cover looking much as he had in *Blue Hawaii*.

We had exactly five-and-a-half days to replace the articles on Manhattan with pieces that depicted Elvis in his mythical life and crashing death. Chet Flippo rushed off to the funeral in Memphis and filed his article from there. Joe Klein visited the two-room shack in Tupelo, Mississippi where Elvis grew up and interviewed people who knew the Presley family. *They were poor all right, but they weren't trash.*

Jann was thrilled when Caroline Kennedy agreed to view the body at Graceland and write two-hundred-and-fifty words describing how "his face seemed swollen, and his sideburns reached his chin." The former president's daughter met the dead king's wife, his sixty-one-year-old dad, and six-year-old Lisa Marie. Asked to capture the scene, Caroline noted details like floral arrangements at the gates shaped like crowns, broken hearts, hound dogs, and blue suede shoes.

Jann edited Caroline's copy with an unnaturally gentle hand, handling the inexperienced writer with unusual patience. Facing such a grueling deadline, however, he barred the young woman from leaving the office until the piece was ready for the copy desk. Caroline took in the entire scene with amazing grace.

Iris asked me to keep an eye on Caroline. Peeking into the office she had been relegated, I saw a lovely slender woman staring out the window.

"Hello," I said softly, so as not to surprise her.

She turned to look at me and smiled. "I'm Caroline."

"Susan. I'm on the editorial staff here and I just wanted to make sure that you've got everything you need.

"I do, thanks. Just waiting for Jann to finish editing my article. He may have some questions."

"Good. Good. Well, I don't know if you'd be interested, but I'm working on an event at the Riverside Church to celebrate the United Nation's admission of Vietnam. It's next week. I have some extra tickets."

She bought two.

"Also," I hesitated but then went for it, "I take care of freelance writers' payments here. I'll be processing your check for two hundred dollars. Would you, by any chance, want to donate that to the cause?"

She very politely declined. But I had to ask.

Greil Marcus, who revered and wrote about Elvis more than anyone at *Rolling Stone,* was the logical person to write the actual tribute, except that he was vacationing with his wife in Maui. One day before deadline, we managed to finally track him down at the resort and explain that the magazine needed a tie-up piece that truly defined the musician's contribution.

"Don't tell me that *Rolling Stone* doesn't keep a ready file of obits. That's a joke, right?" he snorted from the faraway island, admittedly full of Jack Daniels. But he acquiesced and agreed to jot down some thoughts and call back. Several hours later he read the copy to us from poolside. Recording Greil through a clunky device attached to a speakerphone in New York seemed high-tech, though labor intensive. Several of us monitored the phone call to make sure the tape picked up his words. I took down what I could on a legal pad, as backup. Both Iris and I worked on transcribing the tape into raw copy. Hours later the story was being laid out in the brand-new production room with selected photos.

Culmination of the Elvis issue had the effect of breaking in the pristine New York headquarters. Before the day that Elvis died, divisions formed between the newly arrived and the already there. Culture clashes on top of culture shock. It did not take much for Dave Marsh to throw his typewriter across his office. No Wilde's Tavern existed to duck into, to commiserate, to drink and connect. Instead, *Rolling Stone* staffers drifted, complained, and bickered.

On the day that Elvis died, the New York space above Central Park finally became *Rolling Stone.* No whitewashed office wall could block the exchange of rapid-fire ideas and action, real action. Procrastinating writers slid paper into their brand-new typewriters and responded to editors. Jann threw his weight around but stayed on target and in the office. Iris stopped being simply Jann's secretary and dazzled again as the mighty queen of efficiency.

When the special Elvis issue sailed off in fine finished form to the printers, with the forever-young king on the cover, we could finally disperse. Our offices were no longer sterile with typewriters askew on desks cluttered with shards of edited words. Days of take-out food wrappings filled trash cans. Unwashed coffee cups lay about with dregs of caffeine and dried liquor. We had put the magazine to bed.

I heard from Howard Kohn, still in San Francisco, during the marathon production. He had nothing to contribute to a magazine devoted to Elvis but intended to be in New York the following week. Could he stay with me? he asked. "Oh, and by the way, Diana is coming with me."

Howard's words followed me as I walked home that afternoon down Fifth Avenue in the dry warmth of late summer, across Twenty-Third Street, to a deli on Sixth Avenue. I'd done it: worked nonstop on a special issue produced in record time. Exhaling finally, the cut of his words caught in my throat. Still, I ordered a huge sandwich with corned beef, coleslaw, and Russian dressing on rye. Rather than heading home, I bought a ticket to see *New York, New York* at the Quad Cinema on Thirteenth Street. Only in the dark nearly empty theater, finally satiated by the salty meat and sweet tangy slaw eaten slowly while listening to Liza Minnelli sing the song that could have been my love theme with the city, could I relax.

After three months of envisioning Howard's return, I had said yes. He could bring his wife to stay at my Chelsea walkup. Life never does reflect make-believe—I had learned that long before, when my father knocked on the door to take us to *Blue Hawaii*—and now, with the king dead and buried, I was too exhausted to care.

CHAPTER 14

Anxious to tell Robert about the Elvis issue, I dialed his number. No one answered. Sitting back with a glass of wine, my emotions ricocheted between curiosity and a nagging ache. We had not talked much lately. I knew he was all right, buzzing about Baltimore with his many friends. He filled me in somewhat when we did connect. Mom had recently mentioned that he was dating someone.

Girls were always drawn to my brother. Even my girlfriends had insisted on touring his bedroom, their eyes fawning over hastily thrown sweaters and stacked records. But as that ever-so-seductive high school varsity rah-rah-rah faded, my brother quietly matured into a real mensch. He would do anything for friends or family, whether tutoring in math or listening tirelessly to one's woes. Whoever this new woman was, I told myself, she would be damn lucky to have him.

He had, I would later learn, run into Charlene Mazer one day at Edmart Deli and, across rows of bagels and corned meats, saw something new and beautiful in his acquaintance, someone he had known in high school and at the University of Maryland. Perhaps Charlene's porcelain skin had taken on a different glow in her midtwenties, or her long legs appeared shapelier in the cropped fashions of the seventies. Her wide green eyes met his and the instant attraction simmered into a relationship.

I met her earlier that summer in Baltimore when I went to escape the pent-up summer heat of my fifth-floor walkup and to distract myself from constantly thinking of Howard. I didn't notice my brother's brewing romance, nor did he say anything, though the vibes must have been plainly evident.

Robert had invited me over to Brian's house to swim in the backyard pool during that visit. Everyone often gathered at his lavish childhood home, since Brian hadn't managed to move out and his parents never objected to the twenty-somethings gathering there to use the amenities and eat the food.

Robert did not mention Charlene. "It's going to be the usual crowd," he told me. His crowd—Pikesville High Class of '69—remained a colorful montage of dark handsome guys with witty tongues and rail-thin, well-manicured girls. Being among Robert's friends always brought me back home, in a good way. Brian, Sandy, Harold, David, Ducky, Irv, Steve, and so many more who, nearly a decade after graduation, still called me Little K. I liked it. I was working at a big-time magazine, but this crowd wasn't impressed by my job or who I had become. They had too many good memories of Little K.

"Remember the 'virgin' incident," David announced, taking us back to 1966.

Barely a teen, I had recently kissed Arnie, a boy in our apartment complex. Cute and a little wild, I enjoyed his sudden attention as we gathered outside, lighting cigarettes and talking shit. Arnie had singled me out, and I followed him a short distance from the others.

He pushed me down on concrete steps and sidled very close. "Have you ever been kissed?"

I shook my head, heart pounding. His lips fast found mine. His hands roamed but I pushed them away. I didn't want him to discover the Kleenex stuffed in my trainer bra in lieu of budding breasts. Arnie lost interest quickly and rejoined the others. Flush with the excitement of my first kiss, and not knowing the terminology, I naively thought I had lost my innocence.

Not long after, flexing my grownup-ness, I had barged into Robert's room when he had David, Ducky, and a few others sitting there.

"Get out," Robert ordered.

"No."

The other boys chuckled, which only egged me on. "I don't have to leave."

"Why not?"

"I'm not a virgin."

Robert sprung from his bed and called to Mom. "Will you get your daughter out of my room!"

I didn't mind the raucous laughter that anecdote could still trigger among Robert's friends. I had been a shy, awkward kid who desperately wanted to be liked. In my early twenties and living in New York City, I could look back and offer some advice to that pathetic me. *Hang in there, kid. Things will get better.*

Refreshed by the cool water and a few laps, I saw Charlene floating on one of the rafts, her long slender bikini-clad body outstretched. She said hello.

"How are you?" I asked, as if I recognized her. She looked vaguely familiar.

She lifted a head crowned with blond curls, her luminous green eyes on me. "Fine. Just fine."

As afternoon ebbed into evening, I barely noticed whether Robert gravitated toward Charlene. They must have been talking, and I missed it.

Later, after we finished the Elvis issue, when I finally reached him by phone, Robert admitted, "This girl is special."

They were a perfect complement. I saw that over time. Charlene's laughter came easily; his bubbled up slowly. Her spontaneity pulled him from endless deliberations. She resurrected the Robert who I'd thought we lost to the grind of my uncle's factory.

I was happy for him. But I wanted more for Robert than the suburban Baltimore life with its painful echoes of our father's long-ago mistakes. Ever since my brother had swallowed the aspirin in a desperate move, my concern smoldered. Yet I couldn't bypass how his thickly guarded smile and twinkling eyes would focus on Charlene, who became glittering proof that he had gotten up from his tumbles with more pizazz, more strength, more charm than ever. I only saw what he wanted me to see.

CHAPTER 15

Howard and his wife, Diana, spoke highly of *Rolling Stone*'s new public relations director when they bunked with me in Chelsea. They said David Fenton was smart, political, knew how to get the story out, and listened to jazz more than rock. They said these things as I wrapped my mind around the presence of Diana calmly sitting on a bar stool at my kitchen counter spooning coffee-flavored Haagen-Dazs into one of my glass bowls. Nothing in her dark, regular features stoked envy. She licked the back of the spoon. I had never seen anyone do that before.

Diana told me about knowing David in Ann Arbor, back when Howard worked for the *Michigan Daily* and David, a high school dropout, published a newspaper for the Rainbow People's Party of Ann Arbor. She talked far more than Howard, who wandered about my apartment somewhat awkwardly. The rooms must've echoed what we'd had, all that heat.

Diana asked me, "Do you remember when John Lennon helped free John Sinclair?"

I shook my head.

"Well, anyway, David was involved with that.

"David got Lennon to perform. That's David," Diana had said, or she said something implying that David, nervy, got things done.

I found myself liking her more, as she methodically licked both sides of the ice cream spoon while I drank wine, her talking, weaving more stories in my tiny apartment than Scheherazade to the Persian king. Plain spoken, devoted to Howard, unflappable. If she knew about Howard and me, she said nothing. Perhaps we shared that. Denial.

Every time Howard brushed past me, I could feel the electricity. He must feel it, too, I convinced myself. Getting to know Diana had not dampened my ardor.

I allowed the new *Rolling Stone* publicity director to lure me up to the business floor only because Howard had specifically asked me to welcome David to the magazine. I found his office easily since Coltrane poured from a ghetto blaster, and his voice rose above the music, as if the whole world wanted to hear every word David Fenton uttered. Waiting for him to finish his call, I saw, newly hung, the poster for the John Sinclair Freedom Rally. *Ten for Two*—as in, John Sinclair was given ten years in the state prison for two marijuana joints. Lennon wrote a ditty that he sang with Yoko Ono at the rally: *It ain't fair John Sinclair . . . They gave him ten for two.* Seventy-two hours after the rally, John Sinclair walked out of jail a free man. Diana had explained all this to me.

David startled me when he leaped from his chair to grab both my hands like a gawky adolescent with uncontrollable energy. He rushed to speak first. "I hear we should work very well together." When I didn't immediately respond, the smile on his face curled downward, as if he really wanted to please me. I only thought how self-satisfied he seemed at barely twenty-five, barely older than me, with cropped curls and lids at half-mast on pale eyes.

I pointed to the John Sinclair poster. "You were part of that?"

He explained how Jerry Rubin and Abbie Hoffman had masterminded the slogan and the concert. They trained David, then a precocious kid in his mid-teens. So in lieu of college professors, David had two of the Chicago Seven conspirators indicted for inciting riots at the '68 Democratic Convention run him through counterculture lessons.

"I learned a lot from Jerry and Abbie."

"About a drug case?"

"No," he corrected. "How to capture public attention with a slogan like *ten for two.* How to inform people so they do the right things, like pressure the judge to free Sinclair."

David didn't immediately appeal to me, his New York Jewish smarts spreading a self-satisfied grin across his narrow face. Only his close friendship with Howard kept me sitting in his office.

I asked how he wound up at the magazine.

"I convinced Jann he couldn't conquer New York City without me."

"How did you do that?" I leaned in, trying to decide whether this guy was for real.

David explained how he was guiding Jann through a media market that was not rock-and-roll-centric. "This is *not* San Francisco."

That sounded very smart, and I told him so.

"Howard said I would like you," he suddenly blurted.

His words stunned me. Was Howard pushing me off on David? Was I a commodity that could be traded like a sack of grain? Or, was Howard encouraging my relationship with David to keep me close?

Looking straight into the dilated centers of David's eyes, I sized him up. His mind moved fast, like pellet shot. He'd done things, been places. David could climb into a position of real power at *Rolling Stone.* My thoughts scrambled wildly. Knowing Diana was beginning to alter the Howard-romance dynamic. I wanted to remain an insider to Howard's work. David, more intriguing the longer he spoke, offered me a way to stay in the game.

Only an hour earlier, Howard had cornered me in an empty office. He had a few minutes left between meetings with libel lawyers on a possible court battle over one of his published exposes and flying back with Diana to San Francisco. I wanted to pull away, but Howard had paralyzed me with only one kiss, leaving me staring at the gaudy maroon-and-red stripes on his too-broad, too-familiar tie. His large farm hands stroked either side of my head, pulling me toward his chest and into the calming smells of dry cleaning and bar soap. He communicated far better by touch than by speaking. Howard didn't have to say anything. He merely held me, until he gently broke our embrace, and the silence, by promising to return soon.

"Do you like Japanese food?" David asked.

He waited for my answer. I asked him to repeat the question, since Howard's hands had still been caressing my ears.

"Yes," I responded once David's words registered above Howard's.

◆ ◆ ◆

When Jann offered Carl Bernstein of Watergate fame nearly thirty thousand dollars to write a feature story for the magazine, the newsroom exploded in boos. Chuck Young raged, as did many others who didn't make that much money in a year.

David Fenton cheered. Here emerged an opportunity to use a big-name writer to splash *Rolling Stone* into the primetime news slot.

All the President's Men, both the book and the movie, had catapulted Carl Bernstein and Bob Woodward from metro reporters at the *Washington Post* into superheroes who had toppled Richard Nixon. Carl had recently appeared in the magazine's Random Notes section in an Annie Leibovitz every-picture-tells-a-story photograph. The fast-black eyes of Linda Ronstadt ran all over the reporter, not at all a Dustin Hoffman look-alike; from her mouth:

"Oh, you must be *All the President's Men.*"

Rumors were that Carl's new story broke open how the most powerful news media carried out assignments in cahoots with CIA spooks. David, who I had begun spending a fair amount of time with, convinced me this was a dynamite story since Carl's findings speared two evil forces: a corrupt intelligence agency and a despotic media establishment. David rattled off some of the findings and I listened, as I always listened to David at that time, with amusement at how enthralled he was with his own words.

David's seduction of me mimicked Fielding's rambunctious Tom Jones high on weed and with more vigor than savoir faire. I let him chase me because I enjoyed the action and genuinely liked him—and his vision. David and Howard were often conspiring on their shared strategies for a better world. It grew clear that I could have a role, with the dimensions just starting to form. I saw myself as Anna Wulf from Doris Lessing's *The Golden Notebook*, in South Africa, blending with powerful men to fight for an end to apartheid.

I drifted ever farther from my chances at writing on music, seeing instead a higher calling in using my position at the magazine to sway the scales of justice. Gloria largely encouraged my political growth but was skeptical that such development could be fully achieved at *Rolling Stone.* Caught in the moment, I held out hope, based on things David told me, that Carl Bernstein had written something politically potent enough to earn his outrageous fee. David immediately began plotting how the CIA story would be embargoed and clandestinely delivered to influential editors, who would be carefully instructed on when to release the story.

"Will the embargo work?" I asked David. He had called me up to his office on a Friday afternoon without explanation.

"You may find out." He smiled enticingly. "Any plans for Sunday?"

Curious and strangely excited, I said I was on board. He told me my mission would be to show up early at *Rolling Stone* on Sunday morning and receive multiple copies of the embargoed story from Carl. I would then taxi to JFK airport and take a shuttle to Washington. David would notify such journalists as Bob Woodward and Ben Bradlee at the *Washington Post* to expect my phone call. He assured me they would all meet me to receive the manuscript. Even not knowing what Carl had discovered or any of the juicy details, I felt somewhat certain that such a famous journalist had gotten the scoop. I so very badly wanted to deliver a political bomb in Washington.

How fun to walk into the *Rolling Stone* office on a Sunday morning and find Carl's wife, the writer Nora Ephron, at the copier machine as pages of the final manuscript spit out in slow coughs and fell to the floor. "Good morning," Nora said cheerfully through her famous toothy smile. Moments later I was sitting on the carpet with Nora, Carl, and David, all of us collating the manuscripts and stuffing them into marked envelopes.

I had a plane to catch. Though only the courier, I saw my role as more secret agent. Gripped in my arms would be the latest exposé by Carl Bernstein. Top journalists were anxiously awaiting my phone call.

"Should I use my real name?"

"Yes," David sputtered. "Of course you'll use your name."

David had arranged every detail, from my points of contact to what I would say. He had precalled everyone, so I had nothing to fill in except for my time of delivery and my name, my real name. Still, anything could intercept my mission. Would the CIA be watching me? David lent me his leather briefcase to hide my top-secret cargo on the airplane. I felt very adult, but I should have worn black. If followed, I could more easily slip into the shadows. Convinced the story would sever a nerve in the Washington body, David told me to stay in close touch, feed him media responses, and to not turn the package over to anyone who had not been preapproved. Fully programmed to operate on remote command, I left, David holding my arm, coaxing me to go but also to come back. He would make me dinner later, with wine.

"What if I don't make it back? Suppose the CIA finds out what I'm doing. Suppose I get kidnapped?"

David laughed, but it was my safety at stake, not his.

"Just take a taxi to my place. I'll have some food heating on the stovetop while you fill me in on the details."

"If you don't hear from me, call the police."

"I'll be waiting for you," David said as he released my arm. And I felt something, though I didn't know quite what.

Shortly after I landed in Washington, I grabbed a taxi outside National Airport and got dropped by a phone booth at the corner of L Street and Fifteenth, directly across the street from the *Washington Post*. There I made my first contact, the metro news desk. "Bob Woodward, please."

A female voice: "He's not here today. Can I take a message?"

The street scene outside the booth was noisy with cars. Had I heard her correctly? This had all been so carefully planned. "Bob Woodward. I believe he's awaiting my call."

"Miss. As I said, Bob is not here today. It's Sunday and he's home. Can anyone else help you?"

I pressed my palm against the glass enclosure of the phone booth and watched the throbbing of my knuckles, knew I was now off-script. "Yes, please. I have a package from Carl Bernstein. He specifically wanted me to give it to Bob. It's a big story, embargoed until tomorrow."

I had read most of the article on the flight down, mesmerized by what had been dredged up. Journalists on the CIA payroll. Clandestine activities undertaken by these reporters in foreign countries. And the major culprits of this spy ring were the *New York Times*, CBS, and Time, Inc. This article would send shockwaves through an unknowing public, I naively assumed.

I heard a hand muffling the phone receiver, and her voice yelling across the newsroom. A moment or two later, she said, "Two reporters will meet you."

So rather than Bob Woodward, two eager young cub reporters from the *Post* shook my hand. One White, one Black; both young and snide.

"Ha," said the Black one, as he took my precious parcel marked for the other half of the Watergate team. "We were wondering what Carl was up to."

"I guess we'll find out," said his White colleague.

"You'll give that to Bob Woodward, right?"

"Sure will." But they were laughing as I grabbed another cab and gave the driver the address on N Street where Ben Bradlee lived with his wife, Sally Quinn.

Georgetown seemed swankier than when I had visited there in my younger years to hear music, buy high leather boots before college, and walk into stores that sold rolling papers and bongs. When Robert lived in College Park, I would meet him and Faye at Blues Alley for jazz on weekends when Mom let me have the car. How cool I felt on those excursions. On this mission, I felt out of place. Walking on the narrow streets of historic cobblestones, the sleek lines of Georgetown brick and wooden row houses painted in many colors gave off a very upscale vibe. But I kept walking. The Bradlee-Quinn house took up a full block, with so many different entrances that I couldn't figure out which door knocker to grab. Yet the one I lifted and dropped against a shiny bronze circlet did bring the elegant gentleman to the door.

"Hello," Ben Bradlee said kindly but did not invite me in.

"I think you were expecting this from Carl Bernstein." I held out the envelope with the magazine's logo.

"From *Rolling Stone?*" Quizzical, as if he didn't know anything about the magazine or my mission.

"It's a breaking story on CIA ties to the media. Carl wanted you to have it today since you might want to put something in tomorrow's paper."

"How interesting. I'll try to read it."

"It's a big story."

The *Post*'s executive editor smiled at me, that upper lip perfectly arched. "Yes," he said, followed by "Good day then." And the door closed.

I felt the sun on my back, then in my eyes, as I walked in circles toward M Street in search of a telephone to call David. Though laid out alphabetically, Washington meanders like a labyrinth. I walked into the first phone booth I found and rang for the operator. The phone clicked a few times at the other end before a familiar voice answered and accepted my collect call.

"Pony! What an adventure you're having. I came in to get some work done and David told me where you'd gone. This is exactly the kind of thing you should be doing at this point in your life. Getting down to Washington. Meeting people."

"But Gloria—"

"Yes, I know, I've read Carl's article. He hasn't written anything we didn't already know. Every journalist conversed regularly with the CIA in Vietnam. Just like reporters did with the OSS during the Second World War. Our intelligence people knew things we wanted to know, and they knew we had America's ear."

The snap of her cigarette lighter sent a small roar across the wires. "Just because his story reveals nothing new doesn't mean taking it to Washington isn't a great adventure for you."

I could hear the dragon breath of her exhale as she punctured my inflated sense of purpose. "And another thing, Pony," she went on, "patriotism used to be a shared honor between reporters and spies."

Refusing to give up my mission, I caught another taxi. "National Press Club," I told the driver.

My luck in stirring up enthusiasm for Carl's exposé did not improve among the Washington bureau for big-city papers. *CIA? Do we have a relationship with the CIA? Gee, I better read this.*

Wandering the halls of that old fourteen-story news building, a hallowed place with more legend than life on that particular day,

I searched among the scant Sunday shift at men dozing atop their typewriters or gathered around a TV watching sports. I passed out the envelopes to the names on my list until I had emptied David's briefcase.

"Is Bernstein writing record reviews now?" one punkish wire-service guy asked. "Cool. Really cool."

Had I done anything to change the world after delivering Carl's embargoed story to all the right people? Gloria was probably right; this piece would not bring down anything. Even so, I still imagined myself a part of something big.

New York City reached up from below and embraced me as the plane prepared for descent. Energy surges at being back in the Big Apple propelled me out of the airport. On my way to David's apartment, carrying only the empty briefcase, I felt a hard-to-define excitement trickling down my legs. And when David opened the door to his apartment, I nearly whirled into his arms.

He hesitated, then told me how he had gotten through to Bob Woodward and the *Post* would run a story in the Monday paper.

"Really?"

"You got the article to Washington. That's the important part."

"But *you* talked to Woodward."

"Only after he read the story that *you* hand delivered."

We barely made it into his bedroom before his hands ripped at my clothes.

The last thing I remember David saying: "We were successful today. What a brilliant plan I devised."

CHAPTER 16

David's endless talk crowded my head. Never how to overthrow the government, like they chanted in the sixties; rather, he wanted to win over America by plugging into the new era of mass communications and popular culture.

"But when you're ahead of conventional journalists, you're blocked by the press," he bemoaned.

I turned on my side, nearly wishing I still smoked. But he hardly seemed to notice I had turned away. David just chugged along with whatever he was saying like the little engine that could. And I always turned back toward him because I knew those loud clanking wheels were going somewhere. Although I thought him a rude, arrogant rabble-rouser, David had genius.

"We need to hit harder. Reach more people. No one read Mike Aron's story on the Clamshell Alliance and the Seabrook antinuclear protests in the last issue. How many letters came in on that story?"

"Not many."

"We need to make the dangers of radioactivity impossible to ignore."

"Did you learn these strategies from Jerry Rubin and Abbie Hoffman?"

He shook off the covers. "Do you really still see Rubin and Hoffman as counterculture heroes?"

I shrugged. I did but wouldn't tell him so. Despite Abbie being underground, gone, and Jerry an entrepreneur, rich, I still envisioned them wrapped in American flags, beards dark and overgrown, black eyes piercing.

"Anyway, it was Marshall McLuhan who encouraged social change activists to be entertaining enough for the revolution to play on TV."

"David," I broke in, "I need to get out of the city."

"What?" He looked at me for the first time that morning.

"I need to breathe fresh air."

No response, at first. His brain worked in mysterious ways, and I watched his silence simmer, reach boiling point. Then he exclaimed, "Yes!"

Suddenly it was his idea to get out of the city. He formulated a plan. "We'll head up to the Montague commune next weekend when Howard and Diana are back and visit the boys."

By *boys*, he meant Sam Lovejoy and Harvey Wasserman, interviewed recently in Mike Aron's article. Maybe the story didn't arouse the public, as David insisted, but I closely read Mike's details on how the antinuclear fervor stirred up on their commune in Western Massachusetts had ultimately led to that powerful cry, *No Nukes,* and to amazing acts of civil disobedience in Seabrook, New Hampshire, where two thousand people had protested construction of a nuclear power plant several months earlier. No violence at all. The demonstrators just laid down and let the police drag them off, even those in wheelchairs.

Just imagining being at that sixty-acre farm on rolling valleys in the foothills of the Berkshires drew me out of bed, renewed. I had never seen the commune or met any of the people, but legends of its origins and its occupants were the subject of books and magazine articles, even films. The Montague Farm commune got its start in '68 when student radicals decided to flee the city chaos for a more tranquil environment from which to push for an overthrow of the government. Early commune members, like Harvey, had worked for the Liberation News Service and tried to publish there until the ink froze in the mimeograph machine one winter. Others, like Sam, came several years before a nuclear power plant would be auspiciously sited for Montague, only miles from the commune.

"Where will we stay?"

David stumbled out of bed, looked out his window at the city coming alive and, energized, smiled before answering me. "We'll stay on the commune of course."

◆ ◆ ◆

Howard headed down the five flights from my apartment carrying bags for our journey but quickly returned, still carrying the bags. His features were blurred in vacant confusion. "It's not there," he said, as if lamenting the loss of a shoe.

"Did you lose the car?" Diana asked. "Maybe you forgot where you parked it." They had flown in the previous evening from San Francisco and rented a car at the airport.

"I know where I parked it last night," he insisted, mouth puckered to one side. "It's not there."

The rental car had indeed vanished, but a clue appeared on the street sign above where the car was last seen: *NO PARKING 6 a.m.–8 p.m.* It was after 8 o'clock. The city had the car under lock and key.

Diana merely shrugged. Married to a great journalist, she took his faults in stride.

A cab ride and one hundred dollars later, Howard drove the freed rental out the metal-link gate and toward David's apartment. I had called him before we left Chelsea to say we would be late.

Pure amusement dappled David's face as he got into the car. "Can't take this country boy to the city," David said, swiping Howard's head as he joined me in the back seat. "You don't park where they tell you not to in New York, not in this revenue-hungry town. They see guys like you coming and put signs up, just knowing you won't read them. Just knowing you'll be fool enough to leave your car right where they can come along with tow trucks and drag it off. So how long did it take you to figure out you got snookered?"

Howard merely smiled, that slightly distant yet all-knowing smile of someone able to float above the trivial. David's banter barely touched him. Only words, weightless bubbles from a child's wand. How many times had I wished for Howard's ability to simply blank out David?

David's attention span, shorter than the car radio's AM spectrum, switched fast from the towed car to our excursion. "Man, we're going to be with the hippies in Montague in a few hours. Just communing with nature." He kicked his bag. "Brought the weed with me in case they don't grow the right crops on those fields."

Then he noticed me. "You look ready for the hills," he remarked, eyes mostly on where my bottom imprinted the car's plastic upholstery. "I like those tight pants."

They were just Levi's from Canal Street. I hadn't even had time to wash them and soften the thick, dark denim. The stiffness of the fabric tightened across my midriff and derriere, much trimmer now that I'd been running regularly and cut out ice cream. I hated that Diana could eat ice cream every night and never bulge out.

"You remembered everything, didn't you?" David asked. He meant my diaphragm, and my brain belly-flopped.

I slid low in the plastic seat and shook my head.

The last-minute scurry over the lost car had given me little time to finish packing. I'd thrown things haphazardly into my well-worn backpack and didn't remember to pull anything from beneath the bathroom sink. I had a toothbrush, hairbrush, and nothing else but a change of clothes.

"You're joking, right?" David said.

Faintly, "No."

David loudly yelled up to the front seat. "Howard, turn the car around. Susan has forgotten something very important."

We were moving bumper-to-bumper through the Bronx, inching our way toward the Taconic Parkway. Diana turned around and stared. "I don't care what she's left. We're not driving back. We told the commune folk we'd be there for lunch, and we already lost an hour with this towed car."

"Then I can't have sex this weekend," David whined.

"Be creative," Diana said, before turning back to her husband.

If I were with Howard, I would have remembered the diaphragm.

◆　◆　◆

Meeting the gang at the Montague commune dispelled any notion that I had somehow imagined a growing antinuclear sentiment. From that organic acreage, a mass movement had firmly rooted, insistent that nuclear power would be stopped, person-by-person, town-by-town. There in Western Massachusetts, on acreage as pristine as I had ever seen, the sixties had transitioned into the seventies, from antiwar to antinuke.

Ebullient, with a mouthful of tumbling words, Sam Lovejoy was the first one I noticed, being wrapped in one of his big hugs before I could even say howdy to the others. And I knew of his exploits, toppling the local weather tower on a would-be nuclear power site and then turning himself in to Montague authorities on George Washington's birthday—"I cannot tell a lie." He won his court case on a technicality. And the Green Mountain Post Films' *Lovejoy's Nuclear War* had transformed him into a folk hero by letting Sam tell his story to the camera, Arlo Guthrie style.

As we headed to lunch, Sam talked faster than anyone else, through a chipped tooth and a cigarette butt. His reddish-blond hair fell in dirty strands to his shoulders. His girlfriend, Janice, had prepared the food, mostly vegetables from the fields mixed in a giant wok with tofu and dark Tamari sauce. We ate with forks, fingers, and chopsticks out of many colors of bowls and plates. Eat and talk, mouths in constant motion.

I was too jittery to eat very much and too nervous to talk, since everyone else knew so much and spoke so quickly. The smells of the wood stove and baking were intoxicating. All the vast amounts of information being said overwhelmed me.

Harvey Wasserman, called Sluggo (from the comic strip *Nancy*) by nearly everyone, appeared the most thoughtful, listening intently as everyone else spoke. Sam relayed the latest tactics on Seabrook. Anna Gyorgy talked about the growing international No Nukes movement and filmmakers Daniel Keller and Chuck Light said they had reels of footage that captured the recent demonstrations. But Sluggo mostly just ate, peeling off a huge chunk of bread to soak up the brown liquid at the bottom of his bowl.

Sam's effervescence could be blinding. Sluggo, more in the shadows, intrigued me. I wondered how much he had quietly masterminded.

"We learned during the Vietnam War that citizen action does bring about change," Sam said. "Now we're reviving citizen action, and it's largely being led by the same activists from the late sixties."

Sluggo explained how these former antiwar activists find the same kinds of cover-ups, lies, vested corporate interests, and inhumanity involved in nuclear power as they had in the Vietnam War.

"What's different, though," Anna intervened, "is that the antinuclear movement is not dominated by bull-headed men. People who do the work make the decisions. We learned many hard lessons about being a woman during antiwar days. And, before that, through civil rights."

"But what all these movements have in common," said Sluggo, "is the power of people, especially collective civil disobedience. These tactics broke through racial barriers in the South and raised the social cost of the Vietnam War to the point where policymakers had to take notice."

Sluggo spoke directly to Howard and David—he had known both in Ann Arbor. "We are working very locally. But we've formed a network across the country and overseas. It's just a matter of time before something happens that forces Washington to notice."

"An accident?" I asked.

Sluggo shoved aside his empty bowl. "I hope not. I hope we can open people's eyes before one of these nukes blows up or melts down. I'm thinking we need to make a bigger statement. We're acting locally. But we need to be seen and heard on a national level, everyone spreading the same message."

Sluggo stood. "We can talk more tonight. Let's get you guys settled. Howard and Diana have a room upstairs in the main house." He looked straight at me. I saw a greenish glint dance behind his wire-rimmed glasses. "And I'm taking David and Susan to the honeymoon cottage."

I took this as humor, especially since David and I had been squabbling since we arrived. Laughing, I followed Sluggo and David to where we would sleep. This so-called honeymoon cottage was an outbuilding on the far edge of the hay pasture without electricity or a bed. Stacks of old musty sleeping bags were piled together to resemble a sleeping space. "You'll have the best view of the sunrise," Sluggo said, as he handed each of us a flashlight. "Just watch out for the spiders."

"I hate spiders," David declared. "I can't sleep here."

Sluggo wrapped David tight in his flannel arms. "You haven't changed at all, Fenton."

I wanted to disconnect myself from David, show these brave activists that I had guts. "Oh, David," I muttered. "The spiders won't hurt us."

Sluggo headed out, saying over his shoulder, "I'm leaving you two love birds to work all that out amongst yourselves."

Alone with only David in the musty structure, I had to face my lover far from the urban sidewalks. Nature befuddled him. The afternoon sun poured in through smudged windows, disclosing a different kind of person. He seemed lost, uncertain, almost without words, until:

"You really forgot your diaphragm?"

I nodded.

"Well, then."

It seemed my cue to do something. Afternoon delight? We *were* in the honeymoon cottage. Without my city heels, I had farther to reach upward, toward his cool smile. But I stood on tiptoes in sneakers that I used for running and slid my tongue across his lips. We eventually fell into the heap of sleeping bags and touched one another in slow, deliberate caresses. Stripped of clothes, we lay in a bundle of quilted bags, the cold valley air hovering around us. Our bodies together produced a warm comforting shell in which we could both forget about nukes and spiders. Entwining and touching in such an environment, I felt at peace with this strange relationship. But the mood, the moment, fell faster than Sam's toppled tower when David suddenly declared that he needed a bathroom.

Only an outhouse sat several yards back toward the main house. Looking at David's pained expression, I tried to be comforting. "It's just a privy without a flush."

He dressed and trundled slowly outside, as if there were landmines. I threw back on my jeans and sweater and followed him. Just in case. I could also look to see if I could spot Howard.

Once outside, I saw many commune members spread throughout the fields, some weeding in the strawberry patch and others digging for root crops like potatoes, beets, and carrots. I spotted Howard with a large hoe in his strong hands breaking up a new patch for garlic, he explained to me when I caught up to him. David would have to find his own way out of the outhouse. Howard showed me how to throw the hoe so it split the solid ground in a fell swoop. He did it again and again, opening the brown earth to reveal crumbling soil and rocks. It took amazing force to open the ground like Howard could. But Howard knew the rigors of hard work. He loved the idea of growing life, edible things, from well-tilled soil. Holding out a worm, he explained that this was a sign of the soil's health, aeration by hundreds of such slithering creatures.

"What are you doing with that snake," David said as he approached with some trepidation.

Howard laughed. I half smiled. But Howard dropped the worm and conferred with David, as they always did. "Sluggo really wants *Rolling Stone* to step up to the plate," he whispered.

David nodded. "Well, if they'd wanted something from us they should have considered modern plumbing."

"Didn't they like Mike Aron's article?" I asked, trying to stay in the conversation.

"They need money."

The utopian landscape surrounding us turned less perfect. I didn't understand why money would matter here in this nonmaterialistic world.

"It's all the legal costs," Howard began. "They're fighting a multi-billion-dollar industry."

"They don't really expect Jann to fork over any cash," David said. "Do they?"

Howard shrugged and went back to pummeling the ground. I had never seen such pensive motion—intense, with his arm muscles swinging back and forth with the hoe. I could only imagine what he might be thinking. Raising cash from Jann to fight nukes seemed a nonstarter.

◆ ◆ ◆

That evening Sam brought out home-brewed gallon jugs of apple wine that he poured into ceramic goblets and passed around the dining room table. The edgy sweetness felt like the essence of autumn going down my throat in a cold clear rush. I had never tasted apples in this way, so immediately intoxicating. I almost forgot there might be some ulterior motive to all the hospitality.

The talk marathon continued, but the afternoon's skittering conversation melded quickly into a strategy huddle. The commune folk wanted Howard and David's input on how to reach the hearts and minds of people who couldn't comprehend the dangers of nukes. Sluggo asked, "How do we coalesce in a way that shows a real movement? How do we say that our strategy around Diablo Canyon in California, being built on an earthquake fault, is linked to our strategy in the four corners area, where uranium mining is poisoning Native American folk? We need to pull it all together.

"Remember when we marched on the Pentagon?" Sluggo asked. "We linked arms until we'd surrounded that motherfucker. We stood like a human blockade until the National Guard began arresting us. One of the greatest acts of civil disobedience."

"Yes," Howard said, "that was a moment."

"Well," Sam said in his bellowing voice, "we need that kind of moment now."

"We have our martyr," someone said. "Can't we do something more for Karen Silkwood?"

I looked over at Howard. The wine had glazed him, as it had me. I could almost not notice his arm around Diana.

Howard straightened and put both hands on the table. "I've been talking to Jann about doing something for the Silkwood legal fund. Fighting Kerr-McGee's legal team is daunting. Really David and Goliath. But Jann is hesitant. He doesn't want to cross the journalistic line between covering the story and being part of the story."

"But you think he might do something?" Sluggo asked.

Howard shrugged.

I thought about it but said nothing. Why couldn't *Rolling Stone* help the Silkwood legal team? I looked across at Sam, Sluggo, Anna, and the others. *I can help*, I wanted to say. *Please let me help.* Even feeling as if I had been waiting exactly for this moment to spring into action, the words wouldn't come out.

And the evening got later. I could see that even David had powered down. He managed, after some coaxing, to lead us back to the honeymoon cottage, his flashlight wavering across bales of hay and huge trees. "Should I be worried about lions?" he asked me.

"Just coyotes out here."

"They attack?"

"Doubtful," I said. "Your chances of being accosted by something up here can't compare to what you face every day in New York City."

"But I know those dangers."

He did indeed. For all his bravado, David had to be in his own element. Not so for me. The night sounds as we moved away from the big house got louder, and I found unknown noises, deep howling, to be mesmerizing. I liked the darkness, the lack of streetlights, even the sense of danger. Maybe I *could* do something for No Nukes. But what? I would have to figure out something. So many thoughts swirled as I led the shaky David toward our cottage with a firm grasp.

As promised, the cottage's full exposure to the East through a row of high, unwashed windows did send in a powerful early preview of the sun. Morning slipped across the room in sabers of color, stabbing me until I unraveled from the sleeping bags and found my clothes. David, buried at least three bags deep, wouldn't be budged by the farmer's clock. I let him be.

I found Howard alone in the strawberry patch, tilling between the rows. "Wanna help?" he yelled.

My adrenaline surged and the coffee that I thought I needed was forgotten. I followed him with armloads of hay, sprinkling it liberally over the dormant plants. Together, we were preparing the beds for winter. I liked the thought of that, how earth needed covering and I could be part of this simple act of nature. Howard's tilling left a deep raw brown to which I could administer a soft layering of protection against the deep freeze. We worked our way down the rows and then up again, leaving pillows of amber in our wake.

"I like it here," I said, breaking the silence.

Howard stopped and looked at me. "This is real life, in many ways. I mean, more real than Manhattan, surely. It makes you take stock in what's important."

"I think what these people are doing is important."

He smiled but hesitated. "Yes, it is important. The Clamshell Alliance is really growing and they're having an impact at Seabrook. But this movement needs more than local direct action."

"What you're doing is important too."

"I'm just the scribe."

"But you understand these political types. They look up to you. You made the Silkwood case happen."

"Not really. I just wrote about the mysterious death of a brave woman."

I would have said more, but Howard gathered me, just as I had been gathering the hay, in a two-armed embrace. We stole the moment as David and Diana slept and others were not to be seen. We stole away into the trees and all the passion I didn't really feel for David came rushing out more powerful than the early morning sun's amazing spread over the hills and valleys. Amid the burning reds and psychedelic yellows of the unfallen leaves, we lay fully clothed and knew, even as the sun moved too fast into full orb, that we had stolen just the right moment to retrace one another's bodies beneath heavy wool and denim. His clothes couldn't hide what was indelibly drawn in my gut. Even as we stood up and brushed off the leaves and twigs, my hopes were reinvigorated. The magic between us was still alive.

That night, Sluggo piled us into the old farm truck and drove us several miles down the road to Green Mountain Post Films. Two hours of documentaries after more apple wine and more talk zonked me. I happily curled between David and Howard in the back of the truck, dozing lightly enough to hear bits of conversation.

Sluggo was insisting that something had to be done in New York City.

"I think I could maybe convince Jann to lend the *Rolling Stone* name to a cocktail party fundraiser for the Silkwood fund," I heard Howard say.

"That would be great. Getting the right people to a cocktail party sponsored by *Rolling Stone* could raise thousands of dollars."

"But who will organize it?" Diana asked. "Everyone is so busy."

I was now fully awake.

"I'll do it." Out of my mouth, and no taking it back.

CHAPTER 17

After the Massachusetts weekend I told David that we should only be friends. "Why?" he said, as if I had asked him to change the music.

I didn't know how to answer. I just felt differently after the Montague experience, knowing I had a mission to organize the Silkwood fundraiser. And Howard, although that coupling I could not put into words. I suggested to David we would be better as political partners than as lovers. "Think of what we can do to change the world."

"I don't know why we can't *do* both."

I tried throwing back some of the arguments he had been spouting for weeks. "Shutting down nukes and puncturing those that profit by poisoning the planet is so important."

"You really want to stop having sex with me?"

I gave him a wistful look, and a slow nod.

That is how I remember the sum-up of our brief affair. It merely untied our bodies. We would go on to have a far more intense, often tumultuous, relationship as coorganizers and political comrades. We would get thrown into a maelstrom and eventually emerge as very different people. But all we knew that evening as I left his apartment was that I wasn't spending the night.

◆ ◆ ◆

Despite no firm word from Howard that he had spoken with Jann and that the *Rolling Stone* cocktail party for the Karen Silkwood fund was a go, I launched a plan, starting with filling Iris in on the weekend in Montague.

"What a dynamic group of activists. Such ideas. Such energy. Such purpose."

Eating her morning bagel off foil deli wrap, Iris listened. She took everything in with cavernous eyes, dabbing away cream cheese on her lips with a crushed paper napkin. I described what a fundraiser for the Karen Silkwood case would do for the No Nukes cause and how the publicity would be good for the magazine. "You see," I finished, "if I could have Jann's Rolodex for the morning, I'll be able to get the names and addresses of potential sponsors."

Sipping coffee, she asked me a few more questions, mostly on timing, eventually relenting. Iris unlocked Jann's huge steel-plated Rolodex sitting on her desk and lugged it into his office. "You have one hour to get what you need," she told me, closing the door as she left. I sat alone in a room overlooking Manhattan's most expensive real estate and copied down names and contact information as fast as possible. That rolling cylinder contained every notable person even tangentially connected to the entertainment industry. I whipped around that alphabetical circle of celebrities with gusto.

"Done?" Iris asked as I walked out with my steno book filled with a who's who among entertainers of known leftist leaning.

"With getting the names," I said as I whisked by. "That was just the first step."

The second step involved crafting a letter that would let the celebrity recipients know that *Rolling Stone* was planning a cocktail fundraiser to support the Karen Silkwood legal case, and to ask them to lend their names to the cause.

I entered David's office with my drafted letter, pulse quickening. Even though it was my choice to break up, I didn't have his steely stride and wondered if I had made a mistake, if I would be alone forever pining after a married man. I knew that I had no future with Howard yet allowed him plenty of room in my head. His caresses made me feel desirable. More than that, being in his orbit made me believe I was a somebody.

I put the typed letter in front of David. "Would you mind reading this?"

He looked at me, the gap between his front teeth a dark hole in his smile. "Jann see this?"

"I thought we should get the ball rolling while Jann is out of town."

"Good thinking."

He picked up a red pencil and began marking and marking. I stood over him, afraid that if I left something else might distract him. I stood there until he handed me back the heavily edited letter. I read through his scratches quickly. The letter was perfect.

I asked Iris if the retyped edited letter could be printed on *Rolling Stone* letterhead.

"Now you're sure that Jann has agreed to this?" She gave me one of her dark direct stares.

"That's what Howard says," I may have lied. "You can double-check with the boss."

Before the Silkwood sponsor letters went out the door, Howard and Jann might have conferred. Iris signed Jann's name, with or without his approval. David never asked me anything after editing the letter. No one thought much would come of it.

Sometime later, a phone call came.

"Ms. Kellam, this is Dick Waterman. I represent Bonnie Raitt."

Thump. Thump. Thump. What was happening?

"We got the letter about a Karen Silkwood benefit that *Rolling Stone* wants to do and, well, Bonnie would like to perform."

"At the cocktail party?"

"No, in a concert hall." He paused. "She'll be on the road and could do something with her full band on May 9 in New York City. Bonnie has been following the Silkwood story in your magazine and very much wants to see the family win this case against Kerr-McGee."

"A concert? A real concert!"

"That's right." Another pause. "Anything wrong with that, Ms. Kellam?"

Was there a big difference between a cocktail party and a concert? Jann had learned about the cocktail party when his good friend Michael Douglas sent him a large check for the Silkwood Legal Fund and a note to say he would be honored to have his name used on the invitation. Paul Newman also responded with a check and the use of his name. Since momentum was building, Jann reluctantly accepted that *Rolling Stone* would host the cocktail party. Why not a concert? Bonnie Raitt was great. Her new album, *Sweet Forgiveness*, had hit big with the single "Runaway." This blues singer was all over the airwaves.

"No problem at all." Excitement outweighed my doubts. "A concert would be wonderful."

With his gruff voice, I imagined a much older man when Dick spoke. "There is something you will have to do, however."

"What's that?"

"We'll need a headliner act. Bonnie hasn't played New York City for a while and may not be able to fill a large concert venue. You'll have to find a big-name performer who can."

"Sure." I had become mighty. I could do anything.

David threw back his head and laughed when I replayed word-for-word my phone conversation with Dick Waterman. He thought Bonnie's generous offer was exactly what we needed to boost the profile of the Karen Silkwood case. Brisk with me now that we were no longer lovers, he cut off our conversation when I still had many questions.

"Just remember *Ten for Two*," he said, leaving. "Without John Lennon, we would never have freed John Sinclair."

My quick survey of the magazine's music writers came up with the nearly unanimous suggestion of Jackson Browne to headline a concert with Bonnie Raitt. I called his booker and friend Peter Golden, who checked and said Jackson would be honored to do the Silkwood benefit concert on May 9. This pair-up was the most logical option as Bonnie and Jackson had been performing together at a series of local No Nukes concerts that targeted specific protest locations, such as Diablo Canyon in California and Rocky Flats in Colorado.

Dick Waterman was happy to hear that I had gotten Jackson to agree to play in New York City with Bonnie and that the Silkwood concert appeared a big GO. With action intensifying, David took more interest. He reached out to Manhattan's major concert promoter, Ron Delsener, who agreed to take on the logistics and reserved the Palladium Theater, which held over three thousand people. A major benefit concert. All the details whooshed together as I ran on rocket fuel.

Then everything sputtered.

Another call from Dick Waterman: "Back to the drawing board, Ms. Kellam."

"What?"

"Jackson wants an acoustic concert. Bonnie is bringing her full band."

"Is that a problem?"

"Yes, it's a *big* problem. Jackson will not go on stage alone with his acoustic guitar after Bonnie has blown everyone away with her full electric band. And Jackson is *not* going to open for Bonnie. That means he is out. Out."

I left the magazine offices that day with a ten-ton weight on my back and descended step-by-painful-step to the subway platform, slipped in a token, and went through the turnstile to the same F train I took every day. I never noticed the train arriving or my boarding. I just stared out at the moving blackness and occasional graffiti and wondered how I was going to put everything back together again. I sat on that train through my stop, stayed on until the end of the line in Coney Island, then got out and crossed the platform to take a train going in the other direction. I had to get home—and keep going.

In the whirl of days that followed, I tracked down any band I thought would be a possible headliner for Bonnie. This quest took me downtown to the Bottom Line to see an endless series of hot new acts. And uptown to Trax to see Warren Zevon since *Rolling Stone*'s music reviewers proclaimed he was going to be big. "Werewolves of London" was already a major hit, and Warren seemed to be a prolific songwriter and a truly irascible boy. His act was scheduled for 11 p.m. but Warren didn't walk out on stage until 3 a.m. He played for hours, and I left at daybreak, thrilled by his music but unsure of whether he would, or could, perform at a benefit after trying to have a conversation with him. He had no grasp of the antinuclear movement or of Karen Silkwood. An hour after the concert ended, I was back at my desk going through more names.

Balancing my real work with concert production, I rumbled through slush piles and letters in record time. When Joe Klein asked me to do something, I did it superfast. Iris gave me a wide berth to carry on. Gloria pretended not to hear all my phone calls to scout out performers. She had become laxer at the job, especially as her hatred of the Toad reached fever pitch.

Then John Hall phoned. Former lead guitarist and singer-songwriter with the band Orleans, John wanted to come in and talk. He offered to play at the benefit on May 9 but promised some other bigger names too. The lyrics from "Still the One" crowded my head in an uncomfortable way, but I told him to stop by the magazine.

He was a tall slender man with many rounded pieces within the angular, like his smile tracing the circle of his beard and the arc of his head moon-like along the receding dark hairline. "Here's the thing," he told me straight up. "I can get James Taylor and Carly Simon to perform at the Silkwood benefit, but you can't use their names in the billing."

That did not sound like a solution, and I told him so.

"You can let it leak that they will perform. I'm sure that will sell out the seats."

Still unconvinced, I asked about other ideas he had to get the Silkwood benefit back on track.

His smile grew, half masked by his dark facial growth. "I've written a new song with my wife, Johanna. I'd like to perform it during the benefit."

"How does it go?"

And there, in the middle of the *Rolling Stone* newsroom, he bellowed out an island beat touting the power of the sun and wind over atomic energy.

Many negotiations followed: David and I pushed harder with John Hall to get some sort of teaser language to suggest the bigger stars—we eventually went with "Bonnie Raitt and Special Friends" for the newspaper ads; David with Ron Delsener on whether the concert line-up would sell out the seats—Ron said yes, if the bigger names were strongly leaked; and me with Dick Waterman.

"Well, Ms. Kellam, Bonnie likes John Hall, and if he says that James and Carly will play, Bonnie and her band will be there."

Dick also suggested that another client of his, Michael Franks, could open for Bonnie. His hit "Popsicle Toes" did have a following; people liked his folkish jazz. But it didn't matter; at that point I said yes to everything.

CHAPTER 18

Somehow 1977 turned into 1978, and I stumbled backward. I had escaped Baltimore seven years earlier when I left for college. Returning for a funeral took time travel, especially dizzying going through the long blackness of the final tunnel before arriving at the city's marbled Pennsylvania Station. I shut my eyes and pretended I was still sitting on Howard's lap.

Twenty-four hours earlier I had been in the *Rolling Stone* newsroom working surreptitiously on the Silkwood benefit concert and enjoying Howard being in town without Diana. We had long dinners talking antinuclear politics and too-short nights in Chelsea embraced like true lover-comrades.

In Baltimore, I reentered the claustrophobia of a childhood living with my widowed grandmother and divorced mother and the interminable fights between them. Except now, an eerie silence as

Rose Einbinder Krause was to be buried, killed by a cancer that had eaten her away from the inside out. I knew at Thanksgiving that my grandmother did not have long, but her death still came as a shock in January. Such a constant presence in my life, I could still see her reclined in her unmade bed all day watching soap operas and game shows in the years I went from being three to seventeen. When my mother worked, I would often sit with my grandmother on that rumpled bed, eating chocolate-covered cherries and watching the only television in the apartment. I was with her when they broadcast the Bobby Kennedy shooting and before that when eulogies were delivered for a dead president. We did not really talk much, just stared at the black-and-white screen. Being widowed so young took the bloom off Rose. She was barely seventy when she finally withered away.

I had gotten the phone call in the newsroom: Come home. I could only think about red-and-silver foil on the chocolate cherries I once loved to unwrap. Shaped like the end of my thumb, I would suck on the candy so slowly, trying not to crack the fragile chocolate shell and let the cherry syrup drip out. I found Howard and told him my grandmother was dead. Saying the words, everything oozed. Howard held me on his lap as I sobbed.

I shut my eyes going through the dark tunnel into Baltimore's Pennsylvania Station. Gone was the capable woman working for a cool magazine and organizing a benefit concert. I walked off the train a girl again. Unlike my breezy summer visit, this funeral trip threw me back to extended family, to a confined role from which I could never break free: the aunts, the uncles, the cousins, and that sense of being so very different from them. There would also be my mother.

"What have you brought to wear for the funeral?" she asked. I had just put down my bag in the townhouse entryway. Her husband, Ted, was still at work.

"Just black things."

"What kind of *black* things?"

I had packed so quickly that I hardly recalled what I'd thrown into my bag.

"Doesn't matter," she said, "I have something you can wear."

Here was my mother, having just lost her mother and seemingly concerned only with what I would wear to the funeral. Simply put, Annette Krause Kellam Patz was a master of emotional diversion. How much easier to fret over clothes than to confront the loss of her lifetime bulwark. She remained in total control, makeup applied perfectly and no sign of tears as she coolly appraised my appearance. I thought about her phone demeanor when she'd informed me of Robert's swallowing of the aspirin. There had been barely a quiver in her voice as she relayed the harsh facts. Only much later would I understand the toll a lifetime of deflecting her true feelings took on her.

The funeral service whirled by in a blur, a smattering of recollections of a life that had largely ended twenty years earlier when Grandpa Abe died.

"What do you think will be the first thing Rose tells Abe," one of the cousins asked as we wound our way toward the waiting string of limousines that would take family to the gravesite. We were an even dozen grandchildren, ranged closely in age from my brother's twenty-seven years to young David preparing for his bar mitzvah.

"You know it will be a complaint," Robert spoke up to say. "*Gott in himmel. Gott in himmel.* Abraham, how could you have left me down there alone for so long? Those grandchildren . . . *gott in himmel.*" My brother's pitch-perfect imitation of our grandmother's oft-repeated Yiddish phrase turned everyone's glum to mirth. Even with Charlene by his side, though, I could see in his forced smile how much my brother hated saying goodbye to such a large part of our childhood.

I, too, wanted to scream to the heavens: how dare you take away this bedrock of my miserable youth! I felt oddly uprooted. Through it all, my grandmother had loved me. I was never invisible to her. I could so easily fade among the upholstery, laughter, and ample spread of food at family gatherings. Grandma Rose knew I was there.

As she scanned the spread of her clan, her eyes often sought mine. She would always watch me until I smiled back at her.

My cousins asked at the funeral what it was like to live with Rose. Perhaps they should have asked our grandmother the question of what it was like to live with two grandchildren. She had already raised four children in reasonable luxury since Abe owned a soda bottling company that was viable enough to have been sued by Pepsi Cola for marketing a "Pep" soda. Shortly after his death, the Krause Bottling Company went bankrupt. Rose became bereft and poor in quick order. Because bad things strike in threes, she also got saddled with her newly divorced daughter and two stunned children. We wandered around her large house, its basement littered with soda crates. We eventually filled the basement with baby ducks and chicks that chased us around the soda crates at Easter time. Always, too, there were frisky dogs and cats running amok.

One cousin asked again as we gathered by the dug grave. "What was it like? I mean, spending all that time with Rose?"

My grandmother lay in the closed casket now. I had to speak for her. "I think we gave her a hard time," I admitted. She was not prepared for the way young, confused children can act out. One time, after she had a crew over to reset the flagstone patio, I went out and quietly dug my small fingers through the wet mixture of sand and cement and smeared the mortar across all the plate glass windows I could reach. Robert was often sick to his stomach. Both of us required considerable cleaning up after.

In the years after we moved from the large house that Abe built to the cramped apartment, Robert would take lit cigarettes from between our grandmother's fingers and drop them in her water glass. I had once run screaming from the back bedroom and told her chattering canasta group to *shut up!* after I'd taken a "black beauty"— amphetamine and dextroamphetamine—to cram for exams.

I knew what my cousins were really asking. Not what was it like to live with Rose? But what was it like to be different from us?

Coming back, seeing family again, always reminded me how we had been the cousins in the Floorless Flyer. Robert never appeared daunted by the extravagant wealth that sent our cousins off to Maine camps every summer, had them chauffeured around in a Rolls Royce driven by Scottie, and gave them the opportunity to attend prep schools. Not my brother, who stood there at the gravesite with a glittering Charlene at his side—on her finger, a rock. They were engaged to be married in June. Even on a day of such sadness, he showered everyone with this gleeful announcement. How excited everyone became.

Except me. This marriage proposal came too soon after he had gulped down the aspirin in a fleeting admittance that he was shielding an unbearable hurt. Rather than confront what lurked, he laughed it off, showed us all that he had outwitted the boogeyman by parading out a beautiful girl who would become his wife. I hugged them both, and silently wished that having a family was exactly what Robert needed. He had so much love packed inside his tight wrestler's body. But what else was hidden there?

Robert's announcement softened the blow of burying Rose Krause that day. He told everyone how he had shown our grandmother the ring even before presenting it to Charlene, and Rose had exclaimed in delight. My brother was so good at bringing smiles to people's faces. I did smile that day—but with a heavy heart.

CHAPTER 19

Back in New York, the Karen Silkwood benefit concert began careening into reality. With a full lineup of musicians who could sell out the Palladium, promoter Ron Delsener declared the concert a *go*. Once *Rolling Stone* put down a deposit, the concert venue would be ours on May 9, 1978.

"What does Jann know?" Iris asked when I mentioned getting a check drawn up.

"Whatever you or Howard have told him."

"I haven't said anything to him since it was a cocktail party."

My stomach lurched. "He must know *something.*"

"Let's find out," she said, and knocked on his closed door.

We heard him grumble, "What?"

I should have taken a mercurial reading on the tone of his voice and told Iris to wait. But we needed the deposit check.

"I'll go in alone," Iris said.

The angry screams reached me fast. "A concert? A *Rolling Stone* benefit concert? No way is this going to happen."

Jann ran past me. He sprinted through the newsroom yelling that *Rolling Stone* would not be involved in any benefit concert for Karen Silkwood. "I did not sanction something put together by an inexperienced girl who knows shit about concert production. I forbid anyone to work on it."

Still ignoring me when he returned, Jann told Iris absolutely no checks were to be written to hold the Palladium. He slammed his door.

There was little I could say at that point except to admit there is a big difference between a cocktail party and a concert. I was too stunned to feel the ramifications of what had just happened. Everyone's eyes were on me.

"I'm sorry," Iris responded. She gave me a hug warm enough to momentarily soften the blow.

I called Howard in San Francisco and told him Jann and *Rolling Stone* were no longer involved in the concert, if they ever had been. "What do we do now?"

His calm voice attempted to soothe me, but I needed more. We had no money and no organizational sponsor. Howard promised to send me a personal check to hold the concert hall. "I'll get back to you on the other."

"This concert has to happen," I implored. The stakes had risen with rock stars aboard. And the Silkwood legal team was counting on the money. I had groveled to get this far, I told Howard, and was prepared to keep groveling.

"Don't worry. I'll make this work." I clung to Howard's words as I glanced down that cliff toward disaster.

A few days later Howard called to say the Washington, DC-based Supporters of Silkwood would sponsor the concert and handle the bookkeeping. They'll be in touch, he assured me.

With Howard's check holding the Palladium for May 9, David

began talking publicity. He wanted to do a press conference with the musicians, and we talked about how that might work.

Then Bonnie Raitt had more demands. Dick Waterman called to say that even filling the Palladium's thirty-four hundred seats at nine dollars a ticket would not raise enough money to satisfy Ms. Raitt, who wanted this Silkwood benefit to be worth her effort and, more important, to ensure the Silkwood legal team would receive a hefty check—no less than fifteen thousand dollars. Considering all the concert expenses, I calculated we would need to charge at least a hundred people for twenty-five-dollar seats to meet the mark. Those "patrons" who paid the higher price would have to be enticed to do so by the chance to mingle with the musicians at an after-party.

I headed uptown to meet Jimmy Pullis.

Jimmy's two Manhattan clubs—JP's and Trax—were to rock and roll what Elaine's, a notable eatery brimming with authors, was to the literati. Jimmy's clubs provided a scene for pop-music luminaries to watch unknown acts and mingle. In '65, Jimmy was selling cars on Flatbush Avenue in Brooklyn; a dozen years later and he was showcasing artists for record companies.

Arranging the meeting was easy. Getting Jimmy to focus was tough. I met him in JP's during the off hours when the club was well lit and I could see his full rugged form, a man not yet forty but clearly at his peak since the music industry was rapidly transforming and what he had to offer catered to the moment. Intimate rock clubs suited a smaller industry. Newer, glitzier, and more exclusive clubs popped up throughout the eighties and erased even such notable spots as Max's Kansas City and the Mudd Club. But that afternoon Jimmy, at the top of his game, took both my hands in one of his and expressed delight at meeting me. "Tell me about this Silkwood chick."

"Karen Silkwood worked for Kerr—"

Jimmy put up his hand like a traffic cop. "Wait a minute." He signaled to one of the guys setting tables. "Bring this lovely lady whatever she wants to drink."

I asked for white wine.

He turned back to me. "Go on."

"Karen died on an Oklahoma highway. She was on her way to meet a *New York Times* reporter."

Jimmy called over another guy and introduced him as his assistant. "Listen to this woman from *Rolling Stone.* She wants to use one of the clubs for an after-party on May 9. Bonnie Raitt is performing."

"So are James Taylor and Carly Simon," I inserted.

"It's a benefit for this Karen chick, but I guess she's dead."

The assistant merely nodded.

"We're raising money for the Silkwood Legal Fund. Her family is battling Kerr-McGee."

Jimmy stopped me again. "Okay. This is good. We'll do it. I'm thinking the party will start at midnight and go on to whenever. I'll let you use Trax for free. And I'll have the instruments put on the riser, should anyone want to jam. Who can you get to be there?"

"Plenty of industry people and musicians," I replied, although I had no way of knowing as I made the pitch that, in fact, many industry stars *would* come.

"Good." Jimmy ordered his assistant to work out the details with me. "Give her whatever she wants."

◆   ◆   ◆

The weeks leading up to the Silkwood benefit threw me into wonderful chaos. Like Charlie Chaplin pantomiming output in the film *Modern Times*, I mechanically satisfied everyone's demands at the magazine, as my heart and soul revolved only around the concert's success. I envisioned a huge *SOLD OUT* banner slapped across the Silkwood benefit posters and newspaper ads. Jann was right: I had no concert production experience. But I could pantomime.

Many things were changing as the magazine became ever more

ensconced in New York culture. Gloria Emerson finally packed up her office and left one day in a huff: "I can't work for the Toad anymore!" She wished me luck on the Silkwood benefit and offered advice. "Just remember why you're doing this, for the larger cause," she said. "You are a soldier in battle now and it's going to get rough." Gloria admitted she saw the possibilities for change that might occur from nationwide rallies and protests. "Stay strong, Pony. I'll miss you."

I had to say goodbye to a woman who had taught me so much. She believed in me, gave me confidence in my ability to eventually become a journalist. Throughout the years that I did cover the machinations of the US Congress in Washington, her voice would run through my mind as I sat in the press galleries and roamed the halls of the Capitol. *Details, Pony. More important than what is in the housing bill, what is not? Run after that senator, demand to know why he didn't support that amendment. Don't assume the WIC program works. Drive to Baltimore and see how those mothers are served.*

Another blow came when Howard called from San Francisco to say he would not be at the Silkwood benefit. Jann had scheduled a media-circus softball game in Los Angeles on that very day. The bat-and-glove wielders in the Eagles of "Hotel California" fame were challenging the *Rolling Stone* softball team.

"I'll be there in spirit," he told me.

My heart nearly shattered, but what ultimately broke that day was Howard's hold over me. With our affair as faulty as Kerr-McGee's leaky plutonium fuel rods, I had no choice but to bury "us" deep. I finally let go of wanting him, and of wanting to be him. In the days leading up to the benefit, images of Howard faded from my mind as I raced around town, from the Palladium concert hall on East Fourteenth Street to Trax nightclub on West Seventy-Second. David and I also met with Ron Delsener at his midtown offices in Madison Square Garden. He explained about the union labor stagehands and how costly overtime would be if the musicians kept performing. Too many encores could cut into our profits. But how do you tell a Bonnie

Raitt or James Taylor to get off the stage?

My adrenaline surged with every real-time decision cast to ensure the event's success. I was high on the action, moving at lightning speed toward the big night. I could already hear Bonnie's fingers awakening her electric guitar.

Events began taking on very real dimensions. We did sell out the concert and even all the reserved high-priced seats had patrons. David staged a press conference with the musicians—Bonnie Raitt, James Taylor, and John Hall—the day before the concert. I sat in Bonnie's hotel room as David prepped them. Each had talking points ranging from what Karen Silkwood stood for to details on nukes. James was particularly concerned about potential terrorism, how the spent fuel could fall into the hands of the wrong people.

Bonnie, her red mane and full dimples ever more striking in person, gave me a huge embrace. "I'm sorry I put so many demands on you," was the first thing that she said.

"But it's going to be a great event," was all that came out of my mouth. I repeated those words once more for emphasis.

Being in her hotel room provided a window into being on the road as a performer. She opened her closet and pulled out a shirt, low necked and with enough sparkle to it that the spotlights would have something to play on as she sang. She held it out, saying, "I think this shirt could stand on its own at this point. It's been worn, dry-cleaned, thrown on, and thrown off so many times." I suppose that she was that shirt, that lovely draping material with plenty enough pizazz to be outrageous. She'd been around and could certainly stand on her own.

David worked with Bonnie on what to say to reporters, and she asked many questions. Despite her strong facade, I could see she was a little nervous being in New York City and having to discuss nuclear power in a room full of reporters. She *had* gone to Radcliffe College, however briefly, yet was savvy enough to not appear brainy; rather, she was self-deprecating, making so many jabs about what she didn't know, all the time flashing those deep dimples. I found her irresistibly likable.

Each musician spoke eloquently at the press conference, answered reporters' questions without fluster, and got the technical facts straight. One reporter asked, "What gives you the right to be spokespeople on nuclear issues? What makes you think that people care about anything musicians believe politically?"

James responded in his caramel Southern voice. "You came to this press conference because we are musicians. If we were nuclear physicists, you'd have stayed home. Just as you are listening to us now, so will others."

Breathlessly, I stood backstage at the Palladium awaiting the start of the music. Known for its excellent acoustics, the one-time Academy of Music had become a popular rock-concert venue after the Fillmore East closed in '71. Looking out as every seat filled, I saw a rushing sea of iridescent color light up the stately Palladium. Even the columns and walls seemed to glow and pulsate right up to the building's high ceiling.

I hadn't known until that morning about the close proximity of the Palladium to Con Edison offices, both bordering the East Village. A utility firm spokeswoman called to ask if there might be trouble.

"This concert is a political event," she'd said. "Do you think the crowd may threaten our building?"

I tried to assure her that people were coming for the music, not to demonstrate.

"You're sure the concert will be peaceful?"

"Very."

And, it was.

Michael Franks started the concert off with his light bossa nova sound as people arrived. He exchanged his guitar for a cabasa—a percussion instrument of African origin—and played on.

Backstage, someone whispered to me, "What do you want to happen tonight."

So very much. I wanted the concert to be a magnificent tribute to Karen Silkwood, for the audience to get on their feet and cheer at the music, and for me to finally shine. No longer an invisible girl, I wanted to be noticed as a person with some ability and political prowess. But I only answered, "I want James Taylor to kiss me."

Bonnie would be the one to capture the entire stage with her electric guitar and a voice that rang out so sharp and clear that it sliced my heart. This concert, now unfolding so rapidly, proved to me I had the gumption to make a difference in the world—I had certainly changed *my* world. I was twenty-four, and people were listening to me. I may have been an inexperienced concert producer but, despite Jann Wenner's prediction, I had not fucked up.

We cleared over sixteen thousand dollars for the Silkwood fund that night, enough cash into the coffers of the hard-working legal team—all of whom were in the audience that night—to pay salaries and bills for many months. The hard-fought case would reach the US Supreme Court in 1984 and Kerr-McGee would ultimately settle with the Silkwood family for $1.38 million.

The concert also gave Bonnie the acclaim she deserved. She had not played New York City in a while and critics were there, just waiting for her to appear boozy, a bit too sloppy. But that didn't happen. Even the *New York Times'* John Rockwell admitted in his review, "But even if the reunited Beatles failed to show up (not that anybody had said they would), it was still an enjoyable evening, and the principal reason was Miss Raitt. She is a 27-year-old white woman who has turned herself into a really expert blues singer and guitarist. But she's more than that . . ."

As promised, James Taylor and Carly Simon came on during the encores.

James already on stage, the band revved.

"Mock."

Carly skipped in from stage right just in time to chime in the "-ing," grabbing the mic and twisting it off its stand to hold it free form. The crowd went wild.

"Yeah-uh," sang James.

"Yeah-uh," sang Carly, her eyes shining, her long hair tossing.

"Bird."

"Yeah-uh."

"Yeah."

"Yeah-uh."

The crowd was on its feet, singing along, clapping their hands in the air.

Everyone joined in on John Hall's "Power," the only political song of the evening. As Rockwell wrote, "Issue-oriented politics doesn't usually make for good art, but at least the song served as a fitting final symbol for a musically attractive show."

And then everything unfolded at Trax. *Saturday Night Live's* John Belushi was already there when those of us from the concert poured in. He sat at the drum set on the riser, making cymbals chime. Others joined him and the jam session became as lively and disorderly as the concert had been meticulously contained.

A huge bouquet of red roses awaited me with a note from Howard, half congratulatory, half apologetic for not being there. I held the bouquet out to Bonnie, still on fire as she came toward me with a smile of sheer gratitude. We hugged.

"Howard Kohn sent you these." I quickly stuffed his note to me in my pocket, and she took the flowers with graciousness. Yet I could see a schoolgirl's delight at the idea the roses had come from the intrepid journalist whose articles she read religiously.

So much happened so quickly, from midnight until sunrise. Photographers snapping, including one of me with Bonnie and the chief Supporters of Silkwood—Sara Nelson and Kitty Tucker—my crispy brown dress pinned with protest buttons, Bonnie holding those roses.

People came and left, and more arrived. Art Garfunkel brought in his girlfriend Laurie Byrd and then joined John Belushi on the riser.

James Taylor did kiss me before he left—warm and sweet but not passionate. I could nearly hear his tender voice—*Whenever I see your smiling face.* I have always wondered who put him up to it, or whether he simply felt that my beaming smile deserved to be kissed.

As we all drank and talked, the conversation turned to the inevitable. *What next?*

That night made it clear rock and roll could deliver the No Nukes message in a high-wattage metropolis like New York. The artists were excited. I don't recall who said it first, but it got said.

"We have to do Madison Square Garden."

CHAPTER 20

As Bonnie Raitt and friends performed a winning concert, the Eagles trounced *Rolling Stone* at softball. The raucous band cut Howard Kohn and the rest of the typewriter team into mincemeat on a dirt field at the University of Southern California. Jann Wenner said nothing to me when he returned, ignored there had even been a Silkwood benefit concert, despite the wonderful reviews. He mumbled if our paths crossed. Quitting the magazine to continue antinuclear work seemed inevitable. I just didn't know how to leave.

Breaking away from a cultural icon, my first job, and my New York family (or as one former staffer has put it: "our little greenhouse of crazies") triggered pangs of separation anxiety, confusion, and uncertainty. *Rolling Stone* was not the place for me to change the world. The magazine's exit door had already cracked open when Gloria left in April. No one else called me *Pony* or groomed me to become a reporter.

David Fenton left the magazine before me—sometime in late May—after Jann fired him in a fit of rage. David told me he needed something to do, something big, like plastering No Nukes across Madison Square Garden.

"The artists want a massive event, the Concert for Bangladesh and Woodstock rolled into one," David told me at a Japanese restaurant. We were hanging out a lot as friends.

Doing something the caliber of the Concert for Bangladesh or Woodstock sent chills down my spine. But I nearly believed we could do it.

"Bigger even." David had it figured out. "If you're attached to star power, you can do anything, even debunk the nuclear industry."

Working out the details with David revived the strained emotions of our short-lived affair. We spoke with chopsticks flying in our hands, picking up raw fish and exchanging raw words. "What will my role be?" I finally asked. Everything he was saying was about him and Howard and how *they* would work with the musicians and produce the concert.

"You'll have the most important job: giving away the proceeds. You get to determine how to divvy all the money we raise among hundreds of groups."

What I heard: I would not be part of the actual concert production, just the final scattering of bucks.

His words momentarily stunned me. David would not share control of this fledgling concept for a big event. Not with a woman. I had seen how effectively he could work with men like promoter Ron Delsener during the Silkwood benefit. He talked their language, mostly body language. Male language really—the stance of their legs, the long thrust of the neck before they spoke, the wide-handed shake. I could never simulate that language. But I would not walk away. As I spoke with David, I hung on with the muscle I had developed during the Silkwood benefit and made it clear that my role must be significant. Distributing the money would have to be critical to the success of this event. He agreed.

Then we moved on to mundane matters. "What are we going to do about money for us?" I asked. "How will we pay rent, eat, and all those things while we put this together?"

He shared a few simple words: just trust me.

Through all that I felt for David, the frustration, amusement, connection, friction, and fury, I did always trust him. I had no idea what it would really take to reach Madison Square Garden. Yet David assured me it could be done, and that the impact would be enormous. And, he emphasized, I would be a major player.

"Hey, Susan," he said, swallowing a chunk of tuna roll. "We will be an affinity group: You, me, and Howard."

So much had transpired over the past year, between Howard and me, David and me. Could we really work together as an equal triad? Transforming all that had gone before—misdirected passions, infidelity, arguments, power imbalances—into an even merging of the minds would not be easy. But needing them, I realized that I would have to let the past go and move forward with macho confidence. Earning respect as a woman in a male-driven, deal-making atmosphere would involve the equivalent of chomping down on a cigar.

The promised "affinity group" carried notions of strong connection. And I saw David's words for what they were: each of the three of us would be beholden to the other for getting this next, bigger concert up and running. We would watch each other's backs.

If I wanted to change the world, I would have to take their hands. "All right," I found myself saying. "I'm in."

◆ ◆ ◆

Robert married Charlene at an outdoor ceremony on the grounds of the rustic Gray Rock Manor on June 5, just one month after the Silkwood benefit. I headed to Baltimore with an ensemble outfit of celebratory pale blue and white silk. Yet something unnerved me at the wedding, and I chalked it up to a twitching concern that I might be losing a brother rather than gaining a sister-in-law. We had so little in common, the beautiful willowy bride fixing her blond curls as I mulled over my recent resolve, one that would force me to shoulder up to men. We both loved Robert, and that would have to be enough.

Other dynamics surfaced that day.

"I never met your father before," one of the cousins whispered. "He seems like a nice man."

"He *is* a nice man." What else could I say to such a remark? Dad was always an unmentionable at all those family events when Robert and I mingled among the others like fatherless children. We were singled out, I always felt, for a certain amount of pity. My cousins would have heard things at home about Sidney Kellam's unsavory actions. The air was always thick with what was never being said. But this was my brother's wedding day, and my father was there as a staunch rebuke to the years of whispering. He exuded prosperity and Southern charm.

Dad sat with Shirley at one of the circular tables surrounding the dance space, a large grin plastered on his face. He had every reason to be happy. His handsome son, the beaming groom, arm-in-arm with the lovely bride. Also, the very people who had cut him down, thought he would never pull himself back up, had to acknowledge him on this joyous day. Even my mother felt obliged to offer my father warm greetings. "Mazel tov," she told him. "Look how happy Robert is today."

And my brother was glowing, as evidenced during the photo session when the photographer had him stare at his bride's profile. This would be a keepsake picture, emitting profound love and happiness. I still look at the photo, wondering what I did not see that day. Was he as smitten as he looked? Or, had he married this stunning woman as way to shellac his image and seal away his inner turmoil?

Robert made a point of showing me his ring. "See Susan, I did it.

No leg irons, just this circle of gold."

I had drunk enough champagne to share in his joy. "Well, I may do it one day."

"Make sure he's not already married."

I deserved that jab.

"Hey," I told him, "we're going to do Madison Square Garden as the next No Nukes event."

"No way."

"We really are." And I felt as grand as any bride.

The even-dozen grandchildren huddled for a photograph. "Two down, ten to go," one said. Cousin Jill had been nearly a child bride, at least for her first wedding. I remained the oldest unmarried female of the clan. Every Passover Seder Aunt Shifra would wrap a fried chicken wing for me. Tradition had it that I must place the wing under my pillow to dream of my beloved. I always ate the wing instead. As cameras kept flashing, other cousins asked about my father. He remained a curious stranger to them. They could never quite connect Robert and me with a flesh-and-blood Dad. We were *different*.

◆　◆　◆

My four wisdom teeth got yanked within days of my returning to New York from the wedding—less painful, in some ways, than making a firm decision about my future. Woozy on pain pills, I contemplated my departure from the magazine. How could I leave my entire social world?

Then something shattered that world.

"Lyssa is dead," Chuck Young called to tell me. Our former colleague had put her head in a gas oven, like Sylvia Plath.

It had been almost a year since the police found Lyssa hysterical in Grand Central Station, emptying the entire contents of her stiff leather briefcase into a garbage can. Officers had to rough her up just to transport her to the psychiatric ward of the Kings County

Hospital Center in Brooklyn. Since it was August, both her boyfriend and her psychiatrist were out of town. Lyssa's mother lived outside the United States, in Turkey.

When the phone call came in to *Rolling Stone* about Lyssa's acute psychotic breakdown, Chuck took the news the hardest. He was racing to finish a cover story on the punk invasion as his former J-school classmate wrangled with police.

Lyssa had thrown away her house keys at Grand Central, and Gloria gave me cab money to go to Brooklyn Heights and convince the landlord to give me another set. Once inside her apartment, I could see my disturbed colleague in the sheets spiraled like tornadoes and pillows punched against a fragile wood frame. I rumbled through all her drawers and closets to find clothes to take to her in the hospital. But I kept feeling her objects pressing back, unyielding, private.

Gloria told me as soon as I returned to the office that Paul had already gone to the hospital to deliver a severance check. Jann didn't want Lyssa back in the *Rolling Stone* office. They had fired her.

She killed herself in Turkey, where a broken-down Lyssa had gone to live with her mother after her breakdown. But Lyssa could not settle down in a foreign country and regain the confidence of the young feminist writer I had met barely two years earlier. I thought often about the serious Lyssa who wanted to do big things with her life. She had gotten her byline into *Ms.* magazine while being underemployed at *Rolling Stone*.

Lyssa's voice whispered to me, telling me to get serious, to take up her battle for women. I had cracked out of my shell to do something significant for the Silkwood fund. Now I had to push from behind Howard and David to stand with them. During the antiwar movement, women seldom stood on the front lines with their male counterparts. In the seventies, women still struggled to be heard. Anna Gyorgy told us in Montague the antinuclear movement would be different, that women would have a voice. I became more determined than ever to be heard.

CHAPTER 21

I walked into Iris's glass cubicle in late June and asked her to fire me.

She knew why. "I'll put through the paperwork. But I have to show cause."

"Simple. I worked on the Silkwood concert after Jann explicitly told me not to." I felt a lump form in my still-sore throat, my cheeks puffy from the multiple teeth extractions.

We arranged that I would stay for two weeks, long enough to train my replacement, someone anxiously waiting in the wings. Registering at the downtown municipal building to receive my unemployment check forced me into more charades. But this sham would give me the freedom to help elevate the antinuclear movement to a larger, louder, more powerful level, I told myself as I answered the clerk's litany of questions.

Once free to throw myself totally into antinuclear activity, Kitty Tucker and Sara Nelson from the Supporters of Silkwood arranged meetings for me in Washington to start talking about the big concert. Both ladies became good friends and mentors as I navigated this world of activists, feminists, labor unions, and solar energy advocates. I marched at Seabrook and elsewhere. I compiled lists of No Nukes grassroots organizations. Believing I was doing the movement's bidding, I could not understand why anyone involved would question the concept of a Madison Square Garden event.

Then I met Tom Campbell.

Martha's Vineyard was an amazing place to arrive on a gorgeous autumn day. Getting off the ferry onto a bucolic highbrow island occupied by thousands of unwashed No Nukes-yelling youth. "Surely never had Chilmark seen anything like it," the *Vineyard Gazette* editor wrote. Five months after the Silkwood benefit, at a No Nukes Festival at the Allen Farm on Martha's Vineyard that drew some sixty-five hundred people to hear Carly Simon, Kate and Alex Taylor, and John Hall, I finally shook hands with the patriarch of No Nukes benefit concerts.

Tom Campbell found me when I happened to be alone. I had put on a clean T-shirt and tied my hair back as the sun broke through the ocean fog. He introduced himself with a firm handshake and real fire in his yellow eyes. A California tie-dyed hippie with military bearing and a headful of red curls, his fury was epic. Yet as those fiery eyes ran over me, I noticed a slow softening of his wrinkled scowl and something close to a smile. I could almost read his mind: *She's just a girl*. He sized me up and decided I was not a threat. I sized him up and saw my opening. "I've really looked forward to meeting you. You're a legend."

He shot back, "You're at *Rolling Stone*."

"I've left," I explained, "to work on the Madison Square Garden benefit."

He glowered. "Yeah, well, I'm going to have to hear some good arguments before we go there."

I had been warned Tom could shit-can our plans for a big concert as easily as he could shoulder heavy stacks of lumber to build the platform for that day's festival. Tom had lots to do that afternoon, always head honcho at these local events, but he delivered a final shot: "This idea of doing something in Madison Square Garden. It's not my idea. And I have a lot of doubts about doing it. New York City is a cesspool."

Much later that night, after the event ended, a group of us sat down to discuss the Madison Square Garden concept and what it would entail. Sam Lovejoy started us off. "This is really what we've been working toward, being able to get inside one of the world's biggest venues and shout 'No Nukes!'"

David Fenton tried to say something, but Tom cut in: "You do something in Madison Square Garden and the only people who are going to hear your chants are rich folk who can pay the ticket price and don't give a fuck about nukes."

"We've thought about that—" David started.

"And another thing," Tom interrupted, "how many musicians do you really think you can get to play for free in New York City?"

"Listen to David," Sluggo spoke up to say. "He really does have a vision."

Given the floor, David told Tom how the press was doing a lousy job, especially on the environment and health. "Nukes are a powerful industry spewing out misinformation that gets printed. If we attach No Nukes to musicians in massive force, we can use the big-time media exposure to counter the industry."

"Why New York?" Tom kept asking. Based in Los Angeles and San Luis Obispo, Tom knew he could never crack the Big Apple on his terms. He would be negotiating with union labor, not grassroots activists.

"The national media can't ignore us in New York," David said. "They will have to cover the event and the big crowds yelling 'No Nukes.'"

Tom looked skeptical.

"David's right," Sluggo said. "We have to penetrate New York City to get real media attention."

"Come on man," Sam coaxed Tom. "Get on the bandwagon."

Tom's tight relationships with the musicians made him critical to achieving something on a large scale. Besides, he was a larger-than-life force of nature. We needed his gale winds blowing with us, not against us.

When Tom asked again, "Why New York?" Sam did the quick math. "One million dollars. That's why. We can raise that with just one concert and a record album. I know for a fact it took you four years and nearly one hundred grassroots concerts to raise that much."

They hurled that million-dollar figure around like a football.

"How do we get enough musicians to come to New York? You're talking big. Everything big. Except musicians," Tom roared. "We don't have that many committed bands out there."

With each football toss, the male voices rose. I listened, as the only woman in the room, because my words would never penetrate the fray and, by not talking, I could absorb the frenzied dialogue. Learning how these men interacted nearly prepared me for the months to come. In truth, none of us was prepared.

Tom grasped the football. "We'll have to do this professionally. No musician is going to be sleeping on someone's sofa. I'm talking hotel rooms, travel, per diems."

David grabbed the ball back. "We can develop a budget that accounts for those extra costs. This will not be a small grassroots concert. It is going to be huge. There are many ways to raise money around such a star-studded event."

My thoughts zigzagged, from believing we could pull off a mega-benefit concert to wondering if we might be setting ourselves up for a bruising. Aiming at a million-dollar goal was a gamble. Yet *not* trying, *not* thinking big, was defeatist. I looked around the room, at all that bull-headed determination, and knew we would charge forward.

We drank plenty, bottles of liquor passing around and beer cans snapping open between bouts of anger. David lit marijuana joints.

"Who's going to be the head honcho?" Tom asked, glaring at David. Without one, he said, "this event will wind up dog shit on the sidewalk." He repeated himself. "Dog shit."

Tom looked directly at David and me. "You think you own New York because you pulled in a few musicians for the Karen Silkwood thing. But what you're talking about now is a brave and wild thing to do. Very brave and wildly insane. You think you can lasso this crazy into something real?"

When Tom repeated the word *brave*, his demeanor changed. I heard a possessive quality enter his litany of curses. "Goddammit, we are going to need a strong leader," he asserted.

Sam interrupted. "There won't be any one leader. We'll make decisions collectively."

Tom glared; David was pouting.

"Everyone in?" Sam asked.

I held my breath.

No nays were heard.

The whole idea might have ended right there, on an eighteenth-century farm swept by Atlantic breezes. Somehow that night at Allen's Farm ended on a note of continuum. Those handshakes, drunken as they were, sealed the deal.

CHAPTER 22

As concert details gelled during meetings in locations from Seabrook and Rocky Flats to Los Angeles and New York, it was ultimately decided that Sam Lovejoy would be the president (in name only, Sam insisted) for the purposes of setting up a corporation. Our identity emerged too: Musicians United for Safe Energy, or simply MUSE. I liked how the acronym sounded. A MUSE would inspire us. Considering how rough this trek to Madison Square Garden would become, I might have wished instead for a Sherpa.

I gathered with family in Harrisburg that Christmas—1978, a time of year when none of us had to work. Arriving from the throes of battle, weary but also pugnacious, I walked into my father's house and roared on about the difficulties of setting up two separate organizations to pull off this concert.

"Does that mean you'll raise two million dollars instead of one million?" Robert asked quietly.

"No." My screech broke the calm in the room. "MUSE Inc. to raise the money and MUSE Foundation to give it away."

"How about a MUSE Missile to just obliterate the nukes?" my smart-aleck brother asked.

"Leave her alone," I heard Dad whisper to Robert. "She'll be herself again soon."

"That's what scares me," my brother replied.

Everyone laughed, including me. Especially me.

Robert could always do that to me—make me remember who I really was. I was home, in Harrisburg, not dealing with the insanity in New York City. No one here cared about the shape and form of MUSE. They cared about me.

Even though we were Jewish, these family Christmases were special for so many reasons. We gathered as a large clan. Shirley's two children, Barbara and Steve, were roughly ten years older than Robert and me. When they were teenagers, they never quite knew what to make of us. By the time we were teens, a strong sibling bond had formed. When we reached our twenties and our step-siblings hit their thirties, our lives were warmly intertwined. Everyone was married but me, and there were young children running around. The holiday gathering was a time of delightful chaos, scrumptious meals, and laughter. I let myself become the brunt of much joking, not even caring that they didn't take me seriously. This joviality gave me a break from what was expected of me in New York as I became a public face of MUSE, never able to truly relax.

More than anything, these gatherings were a time to be with Robert. He seemed very happy that Christmas, as Charlene had brought a certain calmness to my brother's life. She even insisted they meditate every day. I saw them tightly bound under a perpetual huppah, reflecting together daily in rich silence, renewing their vows with every synchronized breath.

My brother had taken on the demeanor of someone with

responsibility. I received regular calls, "Just checking in," he'd say. His wild streak fizzled out, that impulsive madness that once had him relegate me to a Penn State frat house to fend for myself. As Robert became protective, staid, I nearly wanted to push back. More than anything, I wanted to believe that my brother was every bit as sturdy as he appeared. I never tried hard enough to strip away the guise. I caught glimpses of the shadows but looked away, too caught up in my own morass to pry out what might be lingering inside Robert.

Although I never cracked his warren of secrets, Robert knew me better than anyone. I told him most everything and he was never harshly judgmental, despite hating how I chose the wrong men. The shattering of our parent's marriage had instilled in him the determination to do it right. The family unit became his wellspring of joy. That's what I saw.

What I didn't see was the gradually building pressure in Robert to be an ever more lucrative provider. Just as our father had gambled with clients' money to up the ante of his wealth to keep my mother on par with her sisters, Robert gambled with a fragile psyche to bolster his ability to provide for Charlene and the children they would have.

But none of that could be easily detected during his first Christmas holiday as a married man. Knowing there were stress fractures, however, I might have watched for possible fissures. I knew how nimble he could be at putting on a range of masks. I had often watched him over the years switch instantly from grouchy big brother to affable friend. A real bear when cooped up in our small apartment, immediately upon being released from his confines, among his pals, the high-voltage charm clicked on.

As the Harrisburg holiday tradition was largely a time to relax and unwind, we seldom left Dad and Shirley's house on the perimeter of Harrisburg, beautifully situated on preserved farmland. Charlene let her hair go curly during the holiday and barely wore makeup. "Here," she said, handing me a glass filled with something that looked like eggnog. "Bailey's Irish Cream."

We toasted. "To sister-in-laws!"

I held the etched Wexford crystal tumbler against my cheek when I wasn't sipping the cold alcohol-rich drink. We chatted about this and that, mostly catching up on who we were. She had run in a different crowd than mine.

"This house feels so remote," she remarked, staring out the expansive picture windows to fields, rolling hills, and a distant rushing creek.

"You fit in here." Wanting to imply she fit into our family, my words resonated something else.

She laughed, ran her fingers through errant locks. "Am I really looking such a country bumpkin?"

I preferred Charlene in her more natural state, in sweatpants and slippers as fluffy as her untamed hair. Otherwise, she looked too much like the former model she had been. Without lipstick and eyeliner, I could see true expressions on her face. Bottled colors painted on a dramatic emotive beauty. Even her natural beauty unsheathed in Harrisburg made me feel dowdy in my ubiquitous running pants, with yanked-back hair.

I always enjoyed running in Pennsylvania on long empty roads that meandered through farmland and acreage with cobblestone homes that dated back to the Civil War. The many MUSE personalities cluttered my head as I ran that year. When I sprinted, they jabbered on about who had control over what. I couldn't outrun voices that would grow ever more disagreeing over time. The core group of musicians and producers—Jackson Browne, John Hall, Bonnie Raitt, James Taylor, and Graham Nash—would ensure musical success and top production values. They were MUSE. Those behind the scenes, such as myself, were finely tuned machinery parts—sometimes in sync and sometimes not.

Shirley made a succulent rib roast on Christmas Eve, and I shoved aside the MUSE crazy to resume my established role as the offbeat youngest member of this family.

We had taken it for granted, having two families. Robert and I
learned how to flip back and forth between such divergent sources
of love and discord. With Mom, we mostly had Grandma Rose. The
many cousins/playmates were a bonus. With Dad came Shirley
and her children, something much more than a bonus. Shirley had
been my mother's classmate at an accelerated high school that drew
promising students from throughout Baltimore city. My two mothers
were teenage friends, despite their differences. Mom grew up in a
wealthy household barely scathed by the Depression. Although her
sisters and brother were also spoiled by Abe Krause, my mother—
whom he called Netta—was his clear favorite and the eldest. She
would get up early every morning to spend precious predawn
moments with her father before he headed downtown to the bottling
company. During the war years, Grandpa Abe paid tuition for his
precious Netta to attend Goucher College.

Shirley's home life was the antithesis. Despite her intelligence,
there would be no college. Her mother suffered from an anxiety
disorder, agoraphobia, and could never leave the home. Shouldered
with grownup responsibilities from an early age, Shirley became
well-schooled in practicality. Skilled in shorthand and typing, she
could work anywhere. She supported my father as he slowly groveled
his way back toward prosperity. Shirley could see the innate worth
of my father. She never doubted his ability to rebound from his legal
woes. She saw goodness and grit, where my mother and her family
saw only failure.

As a stepmother, Shirley could also see things in Robert and
me that neither parent ever detected. She adored Robert but always
watched him guardedly, even when he was a young child. I, the more
wayward one, she believed would ultimately find the right path. At
least, the right path for me. She always enjoyed my kookiness. "You
may never find a man you want to live with three hundred and sixty-
five days a year," she once told me. "And that's all right."

Shirley pulled me aside that Christmas to ask how I thought

Robert was doing. She had been devastated by the aspirin incident the year before and never trusted how quickly my brother appeared to rebound. She knew something still brewed deep within him. Unlike my parents, who did not want to see Robert's imperfections, Shirley's affection for him came from a discerning heart.

"He's in love," I said.

She squeezed me tight, just as Dad yelled that we had to leave for the train station.

"Char is good for him," Shirley said, "but she'll never fully know your brother." Those were prescient words, as Charlene would never be able to detect the ticking time bomb inside my brother. She always insisted, even as she remarried twice after his death, that Robert was the love of her life. I have never had the heart to tell her that she loved someone who did not really exist. She loved the front man, the suave actor, the great pretender.

CHAPTER 23

Transforming the paper version of the MUSE Foundation into its human breathing form took more than bodies. Such a major undertaking required a radical spin. John Hall would preside over the foundation board, which consisted of more than a dozen activists, musicians, and writers. Some I knew—Bonnie Raitt, Howard, and Sluggo; some I didn't. Becky Hardee of the Palmetto Alliance in South Carolina, for instance, came on at Tom's insistence.

With the board lined up, I spent hours with staff people from the progressive Funding Exchange learning the rudimentary elements of creating a grant application and setting priorities for funding. The challenge would be adapting those basics for the growing antinuclear movement. How awful it would be to put out materials that might appear pompous.

Sam Lovejoy, yo-yoing between New York City, Los Angeles, and the Montague commune, helped launch the new MUSE office on lower Fifth Avenue with his big personality that winter, working both the production and foundation side of the organization.

"How do I make us sound like regular folk?" I asked Sam.

He stubbed out a cigarette in the remains of his lunch. "We are regular folk."

"But we're also funders. And I don't want to sound all puffed up like a Rockefeller or a Ford."

He told me to write the grant application form with all the obvious questions. "You know, shit like how much they want, what they're intending to do with the money, and their timeline. Then cut the inquisition in half. Make it easy on them."

Some very good sense lay in that simple advice. Sam was the font of wisdom, the jokester, the negotiator, the backbone of MUSE. Although a natural, the Montague activist who had toppled a tower on Washington's Birthday and won his case on a technicality would soon learn that the mammoth entertainment industry could not be so easily outwitted.

◆   ◆   ◆

Deep in contemplation on the right approach for launching the MUSE Foundation, I nearly forgot about having guests until my buzzer rang.

"It's frigid in here," Charlene screamed as I let them into my Chelsea apartment.

"Maybe a tad cold," I said, wishing that I had warned them.

Robert pushed through the narrow doorway with their suitcases. "Ever hear of heat?"

"Well," I began.

They refused to take off their coats.

I tried to explain. "It's like this. We, as in the tenants here, feel the management doesn't listen to our concerns. We're on rent strike and—"

"They turned off the heat," Robert finished my sentence.

I nodded.

"Only my sister would situate herself up five flights right smack at the North Pole. Jesus Susan, it's February. Couldn't you have gone on rent strike in the summer?"

"We've been on rent strike for a few months now."

I made them hot tea and tried to explain how important it was for me to stay here and remain in solidarity with the other tenants, some who could barely speak English.

"I guess we can make it through one night," Robert said.

"How many blankets do you have?" Charlene asked.

"You can have them all."

"What will you do?"

"I'm used to it." As they huddled together on the sofa with their warm drinks and heavy coats, I sat on one of the stools wearing only a sweater and jeans.

"Look," Charlene screeched. "She's got bare feet."

I put on boots before we headed out to dinner, a nice jaunt to Chinatown. Believing the walk would get their blood flowing and internal temperatures up, I didn't bother hailing a taxi.

"How much farther?" Robert asked, as he guided Charlene carefully through the shoveled portions of the sidewalks, avoiding icy patches.

"Just a few blocks."

"You said that a half hour ago."

"But aren't you warmed up now."

"No!" They said in unison.

After more tea and large bowls of wonton soup at the restaurant, they started to talk to me again. I had really looked forward to their visit when they mentioned it over Christmas. But I had become completely preoccupied with MUSE—the details to be worked out and solidifying my position. I tried to explain my predicament to them. "We're going to have the first meeting of the foundation board in Saugerties, New York in April. Barely six weeks away."

Robert looked up from his soup. "Where?"

"It's near Woodstock."

"Wait," said Charlene, "I thought you were doing this concert at Madison Square Garden."

I apologized. "Sorry to be confusing. But everything is confusing. John Hall lives in Saugerties, and he wants the meeting there. But the concert will be at the Garden."

"Who is John Hall?"

"You remember, from the band Orleans." I began to sing "Still the One."

"Got it."

"On another subject," Robert began, "we're taking a taxi back to your apartment. I mean to the North Pole."

I didn't argue.

"Well," Charlene said, "You always say your sister is offbeat." I could hear in the laugh that followed that she did not view my being unusual in a respectful way, as did my stepmother Shirley.

She smiled at me as waiters brought out platters of warm Szechuan string beans and a specially prepared whole fish, its black eyes still staring. The waiter came over and, without a word, used a sharp knife to slit the fish in half and remove the spiny core and extraneous parts, leaving only tasty white morsels. Covered with brown sauce and scallions, the fish was delicious. They both ate well, and slowly began to laugh and talk.

My brother mentioned that work was going well, and Uncle Morty was giving him more responsibilities on the business side of the shirt factory. "I'm learning things."

Charlene asked me if I ever saw him.

"Who?"

"Morty. He's in New York like three nights a week. Sales meetings.

I thought maybe he'd take you to dinner."

"No. I'm not really his type."

She laughed, green eyes aglitter. "That's true. You are family." We all knew he had extramarital affairs during these midweek junkets to New York.

Robert said nothing, at first. I watched him eating, a serious stare on his plate.

"Try the chopsticks," I suggested. I showed them how to pinch the two sticks, but they preferred cutlery.

"Morty is a good family man," Robert suddenly blurted. I loved my brother for defending him, since that's what family does, but I also wanted to wring his neck for staying loyal to someone who took advantage of him.

I understood why Robert defended Morty. On one stratosphere, he knew damn well our uncle did not treat him right. Yet Morty gave him someone to emulate for being solid. Of my mother's four siblings, only Morty and Shifra remained married. Many years after my parents split, both our Aunt Naomi and Uncle Howard divorced their spouses. Being a family man and a good provider like Uncle Morty strongly motivated Robert. My brother set high standards for his marriage. He pushed himself hard to give Charlene a comfortable lifestyle. Eventually, after the children came, he pushed even harder. Finding himself in the same conundrum as my father—wanting more money to be on par with others—he, too, would take dangerous risks.

After the heated taxi drove us home, I pulled out every warm article in my apartment to ensure they would stay comfortable in my chilly bedroom. Charlene helped me make up the sofa bed. "What are you going to use to stay warm?"

I showed her my unfolded down sleeping bag.

She stood there in my heavy flannel nightgown, her makeup washed off her face. How lovely she appeared with her glowing skin, large spreading smile, and wide eyes. I could plainly see her merriment.

"Why are you laughing?" I asked.

"Look at you. You've only got on a skimpy T-shirt. How are you going to stay warm? Did you give me your only warm nightgown?"

"I'm used to the cold." I was afraid she would make another comment about my being odd. Instead, she reached over to hug me—a precious moment of warmth on that chilly night.

◆ ◆ ◆

"Hey," Sam called out to catch my attention, "we're going to bring in a new guy to help you run the foundation."

Only one word came out of my mouth. "Why?" Sharp silent pains ran through me from being stabbed by those I trusted. *Et tu, Howard? Et tu, David?*

"It's only window dressing," Sam began.

"Why?" I asked again, more urgently.

"It's warped, I know. Our funders want a seasoned male face at the MUSE Foundation helm, so everything will be done as they would do it."

"But we're better than them." Many of our funders ran progressive foundations. MUSE would be radical.

Sam wrapped me in his arms and gave a big hug. "I know that."

Both David and Howard assured me I could handle this interloper on my own. I became determined to prove that I could. When I met the "seasoned male" a few days later, he bore none of the sleek savvy that marked other funder types. Steve lived outside the city, which meant a long commute every day.

"Glad to be here. MUSE is truly a new approach to philanthropic delivery," he uttered.

I gave him a desk in the far corner. "Settle in," I said, "and holler if you need anything."

David whirled by at warp speed to offer a brisk hello to Steve. Then he ran off screaming something about there being two concerts

instead of one. "Call Ron Delsener and tell him it's firm," he yelled to
Iris Brown, who had quit *Rolling Stone*—to my immense delight—
and joined our fight. Iris was far too much of a free spirit to ever
become fully immersed in a political movement, but she did try.
Needing to get away from Jann and the magazine, MUSE offered
her a new place to wield her remarkable organizational skills and tap
her vast connections in the music industry. Joining us was a logical
transition for her. Like Robert, though, there were dangerous layers
of complexity to her superpowers.

Later in the day, Sam came by and pounded Steve on the back.
"Another body at MUSE. We're growing more concerts and more
people. Amazing."

"Glad to meet you," Steve said, but Sam had already gone into
David's office and shut the door.

By the time Tom Campbell tore through MUSE after getting off
a plane from Los Angeles swearing he hated New York, Steve had
assumed the pallor of a shell-shocked war veteran.

Steve had ideas about the foundation, and we talked, but so
much had already been done that Steve's role became perfunctory.
He wanted to meet with the Funding Exchange, but I had already
milked their wisdom. He had ideas about board members, but they
had already been chosen. He tried his hand at writing a statement of
purpose that was rapidly rewritten by David and Sam.

Did I intentionally forge Steve's obsolete role? It is possible
that I circled him like a sheepdog to confine him to his tight little
corner. But I think his culture clash with the frenzied, undisciplined
MUSE environment was more his undoing. Slow on the draw, Steve
could never get his ideas, good as they may have been, into play. He
shortly became a part-time consultant. Just as well, since the MUSE
work environment grew increasingly insane. Jackson Browne began
hanging out more at the office and pushing his weight around. Tom
was there much of the time, as mercurial as the musicians. Despite

Sam's best efforts to maintain an equilibrium around the formation of this event, tensions mounted. And the real craziness was only about to begin.

CHAPTER 24

Twelve days after *The China Syndrome* opened in theaters nationwide, a nuclear reactor at Three Mile Island nearly melted down. It was a Thursday, nearly April but cool and damp. The clock by my bed read 5:30 a.m. when the phone rang. "Now people have to listen to us." It was David. "There's a leak in a nuclear power plant in Pennsylvania," he said with excitement in his voice. "Near Harrisburg."

All I could think about was my father and Shirley in Harrisburg. I understood nuclear power too well, about the reactor core submerged in cooling waters and what might happen if the burning core got exposed to the air. I could see Three Mile Island paralyzed in the fog of the Susquehanna and gripped in human error, with two people whom I loved being subsumed. Radiation illness, if not Hiroshima, seemed inescapable.

Hanging up from David, I immediately called their house.

"Dad," I screamed into the phone, "You all right?"

"What are you talking about?"

"There's a nuclear meltdown just miles from where you live. Haven't you heard?"

He laughed. "They're just having some technical difficulties over at Three Mile Island. It will be cleaned up shortly."

"Stay at home today. Don't go out," I yelled.

Of course he didn't listen to me. Nuclear wasn't a bad word in his vernacular. The bomb dropped in Japan was what ended the war, he remained convinced.

Many assume the MUSE concerts that happened nearly six months later were a direct outgrowth of the Three Mile Island uproar. Yet we were far into our planning and well established as an organization when the accident occurred. Three Mile Island only supercharged our activity.

Had there been twenty-four-hour cable news and social media in 1979, images of those three bubble-like buildings on an island in the Susquehanna River would have zapped the national soul. Even in grainy black-and-white, the image proved potent. One-hundred-and-twenty-five thousand demonstrators marched on Washington five weeks after the Three Mile Island accident, chanting "Two, four, six, eight, we don't want to radiate" and "Hell no, we won't glow," toting placards of skulls and crossbones, and streaming banners with slogans reminiscent of the sixties.

May 6 was a spectacularly gorgeous day, the kind of day that led to Frisbee throwing and lying on the grass, listening to the music. Tom Campbell, orchestrating the music portion of the day with performances by Joni Mitchell and Jackson Browne, among others, appeared genuinely happy to see me. "This is it," he said, his arms encircling me. "This is what we're working for, to get so many people together in harmony, letting the government know we're not going to allow another Three Mile Island."

Seeing him silhouetted against the US Capitol in the noonday sun nearly teary-eyed by the sheer magnitude of what lay before him, thousands of protesters—peaceful protesters—and I understood how this was his life. He truly had put his heart and soul into this movement. His chest-thumping bravado merely gave him a guise, an oversized personality to keep everyone in line. Yet he was quicksilver, here and gone, slipping away from me the moment a group of volunteers called to him. He never stayed to hear what I had to say.

Jackson Browne was beaming. "Bruce Springsteen is a go!" he told me. "He's going to perform at a MUSE concert."

"Wow." I knew the Boss was a strong possibility, having recently run into Jon Landau, Springsteen's manager and producer, at an art gallery in Soho. Having known Jon at *Rolling Stone,* he told me that Bruce was interested in MUSE. Now I had confirmation.

"We'll add a third concert, maybe a fourth," Jackson yelled above the noise of the crowd.

"Won't that be great," I told the singer. But my stomach clenched, as I saw MUSE becoming amorphous, uncontrollable.

Foundation meetings grew tenser.

Becky Hardee, with her sharp South Carolina tongue, lashed out at what MUSE might become if we tried to use our funding process to dictate to the movement. "We're going to become the antinuclear establishment," she said. "People already have concerns. It's like we've taken all the musicians and organizers away from the grassroots events and set up one big central control."

Another board member tackled her outburst. "Come on Becky. We're not the *establishment.* We have the talent and the opportunity to raise an enormous amount of money with these concerts. We're working for the movement."

"But that puts us in a position of enormous responsibility."

"That's exactly right," Sam chimed in. "And we can handle it."

Becky twirled her long red braid snake-like up her slender freckled forearm. "We better not fuck it up."

Becky's full fury erupted later that day when her return plane ticket never appeared at the MUSE office. "Where is it?" she demanded.

I tried to intercede. "Let's call Delta Airlines. Perhaps it's being held at the check-in counter."

"What if it isn't?"

Tom, in town for production meetings and to see Becky, came out of David's office in a riled state. "What's going on here?" He stared straight at me.

"Just some travel issues that we're working out now," I said, meeting his stare.

"Then why is Becky not on her way to the airport?" he yelled at me.

"Delta has your ticket," Iris told Becky. And I've called a taxi to get you to JFK to make the flight."

Tom walked a still-fuming Becky out of the office but returned quickly, eyes burning into mine. "You and I have to talk."

I followed his tall back and thumping feet out of the office. Whatever I had for lunch that day rose in my throat. My head throbbed. "Where to?" I asked.

"You tell me. It's your city, not mine."

I directed him toward Fourteenth Street, turning left onto a block of street merchants and loud boom boxes. Knowing Tom some, I hoped to divert his anger through distraction. The street swarmed with activity. Those not slumped against buildings were in our faces hawking their wares. Plenty of female walkers strolled past, too. Tom's attention seemed piqued by this sordid bit of Manhattan color.

I thought about the Tom I'd witnessed during the Washington rally, the man enthralled by the peaceful crowd, his heart and soul invested with them. I very much liked that man. This angry Tom was another person altogether.

"What happened today?" he finally demanded.

"Nothing happened. Becky thought her plane ticket would be delivered to the MUSE office and it wasn't. Delta had it. No one did anything wrong."

"Then why was she upset?"

"That's something you'll need to discuss with her."

He muttered something I couldn't make out above the street noise. Whatever he had said seemed to signal a tentative truce. He withdrew his daggers. I no longer feared this angry six-foot-plus redhead. I even found some courage. Stopping directly in front of him, I grabbed his arms and proclaimed: "I very well may fuck up one day. And you can yell as loud as you want if that happens. But today's mix-up had nothing to do with me."

His eyes darted, transfixed suddenly by a row of mumbling junkies. I wasn't sure that Tom had heard me. I repeated, "I'll take responsibility for any of my mistakes. But I didn't mess up Becky's travel."

He kept walking. "I like this street," he said, more jived than fuming. I fingered some of the scarves hanging outside wide-open stores, thinking perhaps we should head back.

Tom did not turn around. We had reached Sheridan Square at that juncture in our detente, and a bar beckoned. The Lion's Head was a pub designed for the city's hard core, people like Norman Mailer and Pete Hamill. Only a few patrons clung to the bar at three in the afternoon, but they were unrecognizable. The bartender knew immediately we weren't regulars. Giving us a few moments to run our hands across the legendary wooden bar and sit down on stools, he asked, "What'll it be folks?"

"Beer, with an Irish chaser," Tom said.

"Same," I echoed.

The whisky burned going down like a sweet kick. The beer still had its foam when I took a huge cold swallow to massage my bruised gullet.

"Did I ever tell you how much I hate New York?" Tom had just ordered another Irish from the bartender.

"Yes." I stuck with beer.

"Let me tell you something else," he suddenly said. "Everyone tells me what a great job you're doing. You know what?"

I swung my stool around to look into his sun-hardened face.

"I agree with them. I think you are doing a damn good job."

I didn't say anything at first, relishing each of his words like savory morsels. *Damn. Good. Job.* Then I asked, "Tell me what to do to keep the foundation board on track."

"That's your job."

"Any hints?"

He just threw back his head and laughed.

After many years of going directly into the local communities, Tom Campbell knew a great deal more about activist dynamics than I ever would. The MUSE Foundation board was expanding fast with activists who represented sections of the country where the nuclear industry had a foothold, from the Four Corners region in the Southwest inundated with uranium mining to the Black Hills, where nuclear waste was stored. Many more Native Americans joined the board. There was a very vocal contingent from environmental organizations in Washington, DC. Then there were those members with political heft, like Jane Fonda's husband Tom Hayden. Many strong personalities with strong ideas, their agendas being funneled through me.

That afternoon I could laugh with Tom about the many varied personalities on the foundation board. Such levity would dissipate as the stakes rose.

CHAPTER 25

Appeasing activists became my obsession.

The constant need to prove myself as a true "movement" person overwhelmed me. I had come from *Rolling Stone* rather than a barebones activist organization. I lived alone in a Manhattan apartment rather than bunking in a commune or a group house. To assure people my heart was in the right place, I opened my pullout sofa and turned my fifth-floor walkup in Chelsea into a way station for visiting antinuclear activists.

An endless stream of people would call a day or so in advance and simply tell me they would be in town. The most constant was Jayne Loader, who kept a key to the apartment after she had moved to Virginia to work with Kevin and Pierce Rafferty on a documentary film that would become the cult classic, *The Atomic Café*. Kevin often accompanied her. Pierce also became a regular, as he alternately wooed me or, after some drinks, told me of his lovers. Jayne and Kevin were shooting footage of antinuclear demonstrations around the country with a strong narrative developing that complemented MUSE work. Pierce diverged, delving into archival material that produced clips of early atomic testing and of such government propaganda as school kids being taught to "duck and cover."

Howard and Diana no longer stayed with me since *Rolling Stone* now supplied them with a midtown rental. Howard came by MUSE when in town and we often talked. Although his political astuteness proved useful, his shrewd observatory powers fell short on the increasingly complicated MUSE dynamics. He could not see how David's New York-savvy style clashed dangerously with those from the West Coast or how Sam might become overwhelmed by negotiating on so many fronts. As the concerts approached, Howard mostly holed up in San Francisco writing his Karen Silkwood book. Although my obsession with Howard was very much a thing of the past, I wanted his presence during that rough time. He could have defused the building tensions, and his insights might have better grounded me. Instead, I was left dangling, not privy to production decisions but still answerable on those matters with the foundation board.

The worst part of that period was how I nearly lost sight of everything special about Robert. Our priorities diverged wider than the Grand Canyon. He bought, with help from our dad, a small house in a good Baltimore County school district. Seeing his new home, I feigned delight. But as I stared down streets of homes built to a single design, I saw my brother being pigeon-holed into a work-a-day, run-of-the-mill life. And I so wrongly—so foolishly—put myself above that in my single-minded devotion to a cause.

"What do you think?" Robert asked after the house tour. My brother had let his thick curly hair grow wild in every direction after high school. Against his dark complexion and vivid black eyes, the nearly Afro style gave him a strikingly sexy, radical presence. His recent switch to closely clipped hair struck me as conformity.

I looked away. "What a wonderful place to raise children."

"We're hoping to finish off the basement into a playroom." His face turned stony. "That's going to cost a bundle of money."

Robert was basically the sole family earner. Charlene taught at a preschool until the children came, but she wanted material things and Robert could never deny her anything. Taking handouts from our father, as necessary as it became, must have stabbed at my brother's self-esteem. Most of his friends were prospering as doctors, lawyers, and accountants. I can only imagine how hard it was for him to hang with this crowd of guys who never had to worry about having the money to finish off a basement.

But I was too absorbed in MUSE to take much notice.

◆ ◆ ◆

"Your intensity for MUSE is admirable," Iris told me one day. "But be careful. We're working with many strong personalities in a real pressure cooker. It could get messy."

I shot her a quizzical look.

"I don't want to see you get hurt," she said, hand on my arm, "or even disappointed if things don't turn out the way you expect."

Robert had recently offered similar advice, suggesting that I should not lose myself in MUSE. "Don't put everything on your shoulders," he said after listening to me rattle on about what had to be done.

Some years earlier my father had told me nearly the same thing. I had called him in Harrisburg when I was sixteen, one year before I left Baltimore for good. "I need to know what really happened," I began. "What did you do that got you in so much trouble?"

Dad drove down to Baltimore that night from Harrisburg and met me at the Suburban House in Pikesville. We both ordered matzo ball soup and barely dipped in our spoons. He explained all the twists and turns from back in the midfifties that had defrocked him as a lawyer and thrown him from his perch in a prestigious Baltimore firm.

"Investing a client's money was common practice. Everyone did it," he said, still convincing himself of his innocence. "A lawyer had carte blanche to represent clients and their interests. *All* of their interests."

"What went wrong?"

Many things went wrong, as I would later learn from reading old newspaper clips. My dad hedged that night at Suburban House on the seriousness of his crimes. He did not skirt on the why, however.

"I couldn't buy your mother the things she wanted, not on a young lawyer's salary. She had to keep up with her sisters. And I took risks I shouldn't have."

After the court hearings and the breakup of the marriage, my father told me, he fled to Florida and stayed for a long time with a Navy buddy who made him whole again. I had never known that my father fell apart. I thought he had just left us and wondered what I had done wrong for that to happen.

Dad picked up the spoon and took a feeble stab at a matzah ball. He looked uncomfortable, his large frame barely balanced on the narrow deli chair.

Sidney Kellam would never be comfortable in the rigidness of Baltimore, not coming from the small town of Cheriton. I would return to my dad's hometown for the *Baltimore Sun* magazine in 1986, retracing my father's childhood on the Eastern Shore of Virginia. The article began, "Cheriton never was much of anything, just a decrepit southern town, my mother had said the evening before I set out on my journey back." Writing that article confirmed for me why my parents were never well-suited. She wanted to live within societal norms; he might have happily spent his life battling natural elements, finding joy in a bucketful of oysters.

Dad pushed aside the soup and said, "I only have one regret."

"What?" I asked, though perhaps I knew.

"How I had to leave you and Robert. I figured Robert would do fine."

Then he looked up. "I worry about you."

"Why?"

"Because you put the troubles of the world on your shoulders."

I *was* lugging around the troubles of MUSE. Even in the warmth of summer, I felt like a sled dog in the Yukon, harnessed in and pulling with all my might through heavy winds and snow. I could only look in one direction—getting through the concerts—and would strain every muscle to reach the finish line.

CHAPTER 26

Robert called. "Hey, haven't heard from you. Everything going all right?"

I had just settled on the sofa, exhausted and sweaty. The apartment baked long after sunset.

"I think so."

"That doesn't sound optimistic."

I looked at my warm bare legs stretched out on the coffee table. "The concerts are coming together. And we're going to film everything. For the big screen."

Making a Hollywood film was very ambitious, and risky. Advances in technology in the eighties and the advent of MTV would enable worldwide audiences to watch (and donate) in real time to such mega benefits as Live Aid, Farm Aid, and the Amnesty International world tour. Always confident the MUSE concerts would make money, as would the record album set, investing in a feature-length documentary film for commercial release in the late seventies put us on rocky terrain. Movies are great seducers, however, and no one could convince some of the MUSE musicians that their live performances might not translate into gold on the silver screen.

"A feature film can reach a lot of people."

"I hope so." I was in no mood to explain to my brother that many members of the foundation board, who had no say in production matters, were furious at the decision to make the film. I had been listening to their griping all day.

Changing the subject, I asked, "What's going on in Baltimore?" I pictured him sitting in his living room, looking across at an identical room in the next house.

"We have plans from a contracting firm for finishing the basement. A little pricy but we'll probably go with it."

"Imagine the costs of making a feature film."

"But you're doing it."

"Not my decision."

"Sometimes we have to spend money to get what we want."

We were talking across one another. I had no way of knowing my brother's burdens or that he would take on extra jobs at night as computers began to come on line. Robert had an agile mind that could break down anything technically complicated into its rudimentary parts. He would be able to help small businesses, ones that could never pay him much, to computerize their operations. He might have done very well as more businesses wired up, but Robert would never realize his vast potential. He sabotaged his opportunities, either foolishly or deliberately—and no one would have ever called my brother a fool.

◆   ◆   ◆

Mom came to town one Saturday with her husband Ted for a visit as summer waned. She loved to walk in New York City and did so with a certain sashay. Ted, being fifteen years older than her, plodded behind us a pace or two. We'd just had a nice lunch at Ted's sister's spacious and art-filled apartment on Park Avenue, with wine and many savories.

"I'm sure you'll be glad when the concerts are over," she said to me as we strolled.

Conversing with my mother was often done in code. What she really asked was: *When are you going to give up this movement crap and meet a man to marry?*

"My real work begins after the concerts. That's when we give away the money," I answered, but meant, *I'm not going to give this up and live the boring life you want me to.*

"Well," she said, "I certainly hope the pace slows down."

I told her directly that I liked being in the middle of the action. Everything was coming together very fast, but I had a good handle on the activity. "At least I know what's going on. Not like when I was a kid."

My words struck at something. For the first time, as we strolled the Central Park side of Fifth Avenue on a sultry day, my mother admitted she knew how difficult it was for Robert and me growing up in that bitter environment when we were too young to understand any of it.

"Robbie never handled change well. I knew that before the divorce. I had to take him to my mother's when I had the house painted.

"Of course, Robbie tried to act like the big man after your father left. Then Spotty ran off during a snowstorm that winter. Robbie hid in a closet and cried over that dog, refused to come out for days. I know," my mother continued, "that the divorce was hard on both of you."

She had been devastated by the shocking turn of events that upended her life and listened to her close family, who had filled her with hatred for my father. In our large extended family, many relatives did remain staunch supporters of my congenial dad. But my mother had listened to her sisters and, apparently, to her own gut. "I couldn't trust him anymore," she told me.

My mother never understood how all this put Robert and me in a toxic stew, being too preoccupied with her plight and her responsibilities. "I had to be both parents, and the wage earner," she said that day. "You never knew deprivation. Not like what I saw in those public housing projects."

But we still hurt.

◆ ◆ ◆

I ordered Howard to talk to David.

He cocked his head, curious. Could Howard really be totally clueless about the predicament *our friend* was creating? I told him how David refused to back down on his demands to get producer credit in the concert booklet.

"Don't you think he deserves it?"

"No more than anyone else." Getting impatient, I blurted, "It's getting to the point that the musicians, especially Jackson, are ready to hog-tie him."

Howard laughed. "All right, I'll try to prevent that."

But the shit did hit the fan for David the following week. A furious Jackson Browne told Tom Campbell he wanted David out. Out. Despite their anguished efforts, neither Sam nor Sluggo—and clearly not Howard—had been able to prevent David from incurring Jackson's wrath.

I wasn't sympathetic. This latest brouhaha had occurred the day after an article came out in the *Village Voice* that had David conveying how he and Howard had organized the Silkwood benefit concert. There was no mention of my role.

Tom Campbell stormed over to my desk and demanded to know why David had his own office while the rest of us sat at desks in open space. "Tell me Susan. You were here at the very beginning."

Looking over at David, who stood outside his office door, appearing as stoic as ever, I considered our affinity group and responded: "I told him to take the office."

"Why?"

"I prefer working with people around me."

Tom turned to David. "You could have made the office a meeting room."

"Kind of small for a full meeting."

"It is small," Tom said. "So small no one will even notice when it's gone."

After locating a large hammer and crowbar at a store on Fourteenth Street, Tom ripped down the thin walls separating David from the rest of the MUSE crew. His desk remained, but that privacy he had so carefully built lay in heaps of dust, tape, and broken drywall. I never doubted that David would rise from the ashes like the mythical Phoenix. But looking at him that day, fully exposed, I saw a smidgen of vulnerability. He would rise, and I envied him that, his remarkable ability to walk through fire and survive.

I had none of David's cocksure confidence. When in distress, I found crevices in my mind and hid there. Learned in childhood, such escapism offered me some comfort in those insane weeks leading up to the concerts.

Robert, I would later learn, had a mind that contorted like the brain of a highly trained spy. As time went on, he would be able to deceive even the most skilled inquisitors. But my brother could never escape what most haunted him.

CHAPTER 27

A big-time Los Angeles music supervisor showed up one day during the final weeks, walked into the center of our crowded New York office, and introduced himself. "I'm Tim Sexton and I'm going to produce the MUSE concerts."

Exactly what we need, I thought, *another producer*.

But Tim proved to be the real deal. After surveying the flimsy logistical apparatus we had on the ground in New York, Tim flew in more professionals from the West Coast until the MUSE office became a base camp for scaling the Madison Square Garden pinnacle.

The enormity of what we were doing suddenly turned daunting.

Walking home one day I found myself on Eleventh Avenue, in a warehouse district near the Hudson River where I had never ventured. How had I gotten there? My thoughts as I walked home from the office were on overdrive about friction developing within MUSE and the movement. Watching our expenses multiply at a horrifying rate, I imagined how I would have to tell the activists that we had no money to distribute to the movement. That thread unraveled into despair, anger, humiliation, accusations, and more despair.

Facing empty sidewalks on unfamiliar blocks brought me out of my trance. No people, just cars whizzing by en route out of Manhattan. I had to get home. My breathing quickened. What if I couldn't find my apartment? *Calm down,* I kept telling myself as I slowly turned in every direction until I spotted the Empire Diner on Tenth Avenue and walked across the street, hands shaking as I fumbled for my keys. I somehow managed to wind myself up those five flights, one slow step at a time.

No one had anticipated a slick producer like Tim Sexton when we first conceived of the Madison Square Garden event, not in our budget or in the movement concept of governing by consensus. But the reality of so many performers, with more signing on each day, demanded a dictator. Having begun his career with the Ice Follies-Holiday on Ice, throughout the seventies he'd arranged massive tours with musicians from the Rolling Stones to Diana Ross. Witnessing the chaos at MUSE for weeks, Graham Nash had finally reached out to Tim with a desperate cry for help.

Small in stature, Tim carried a very large metal briefcase stuffed with the tools of his trade: clipboards that held flow charts, calculator, Rolodex, and the usual assortment of aspirin, Pepto Bismal, and evergreen Life Savers. At thirty, older than most of us (and paid more than any of us), he grabbed control at MUSE. He ran the daily staff meetings when he was on the East Coast and immediately hijacked Iris, reassigning her to artist handling.

As Tom Campbell had proclaimed months earlier at Allen Farm, a concert of this scale would require a head honcho, or our efforts would be nothing more than *dog shit*. Tom had met his head honcho, respecting most anything that Tim said.

Tim compiled a detailed spreadsheet for concert prep, expecting it would be precisely followed. If not, he warned, band members and their roadies might miss out on time slots for practicing, sound checks, and actual performances. Tim applied a battleground strategy to the MUSE concerts. We now had a full-scale army to supply and administer.

I tried to stand tall and abide by all the rules. I tried to stop getting lost in the city. There was plenty for me to do: my file cabinets rapidly filled with completed grant applications from antinuclear/safe energy groups around the country, which I sorted through and read. How desperately I wanted to fund these people across the country who handwrote their applications. On the other side of the MUSE office, though, constant meetings were occurring where the major decisions were made. Not privy to these discussions, I often wondered if the production side of MUSE had lost sight of our promise to funnel massive amounts of money into the grassroots.

"Absolutely not," Sam Lovejoy insisted. "It's just that we're in the big leagues now. Bruce Springsteen is in for two shows. Graham has commitments from Crosby and Stills and they're working on Young. We've got the Doobie Brothers and Tom Petty." He went on and on, listing our growing roster of performers.

Madison Square Garden was booked for five nights, September 19 through September 23. With no headliner for the fifth concert, the MUSE musicians cast a wide web to haul in a big-name performer, one that could sell out the arena. The *No Nukes* film moved forward with many producers, directors, and cinematographers—and a seemingly bottomless budget.

As for me, scurrying back and forth between party locations, meeting caterers, trying to sell thousand-dollar tickets to the high rollers who would attend those parties, I just wanted the old days back when I could believe that MUSE was an extension of a grassroots movement fighting to stop nuclear power. Instead, we had booked hundreds of hotel rooms, prepared to transport scores of bands cross-country, and cranked amplifiers at full decibels. Rather than shrinking the energy grid, we were draining it dry.

MUSE's dual goals of reaching millions of people and raising millions of dollars scaled heavily toward the former. Yet activists across the country were counting on MUSE to deliver grants that would let them print their newsletters, bring in speakers, travel to meetings, and so much more. Every day I read through the proposals stacked on my desk and thought about how far a few hundred dollars would go in places like the Black Hills of South Dakota or Barnwell, South Carolina. Then I watched that money fly out the door on things like renting sound studios, film equipment, and transporting hundreds of musicians. My garbled thoughts hit high-decibel screeching. *We're going to nose-dive.*

◆ ◆ ◆

My grandfather, D. L. Kellam, died six days before the concerts began. Almost no emotion at the funeral; even his favorite daughter barely shed a tear.

I bawled like a baby. My grandfather didn't even know who I was the last time I had seen him. D. L.'s wife, Sarah, his softer half, had died when I was in high school. I had barely known either of them. Miles existed between us due to the acrimony of my parent's divorce. Still, my tears flowed uncontrollably.

The death of this near stranger punctured my pent-up potpourri of emotions. I had functioned for weeks at MUSE only by corseting my heart.

My grandfather didn't touch many lives, a stubborn strange man. Ida, the woman he left behind in the Baltimore nursing home, was the only person I empathized with, and that was because she was realizing her own mortality. The rabbi favored her, asked her at one point if it was a good time. She answered: "Yes, it was." Past tense.

I sobbed harder. Shirley handed me a handkerchief and squeezed my hand.

Robert sat through D. L.'s funeral with a stoic look on his dark handsome face, Charlene at his side. He had picked me up at the Baltimore train station and talked about how work at the Apollo shirt factory was going great. He said it with a conviction that prevented me from asking any questions.

"Where are we in the concert countdown?" he asked.

"Five days to go."

"Has Elvis agreed to come back to do the last night?"

"He's doing a duet with Hendrix."

"Quite an imagination you have."

But did I have a hard-enough grasp on reality to see this through? I asked Robert that, in similar words.

"Sure," he responded quickly. "It's just a bunch of concerts."

Robert would ultimately be the one to test my grip on what was real, and what merely a finely crafted lie. I desperately wanted to believe in my big brother. At that point in time, though, I could only fixate on MUSE. I wanted the concerts to be spectacular.

CHAPTER 28

September 19 arrived. Sam Lovejoy walked me crosstown to Madison Square Garden early on the day of the first concert to view the huge marquee broadcasting our event high above Manhattan's congested midtown blocks. No commuter coming in or out of Penn Station could miss it, the city's brightest lights spelling out *NO NUKES*.

"We did it," he said.

Transfixed by our glowing message blinking high in the sky, I had no words. Although brimming with apprehension about what had to be done, I stood there that morning and saw what we had accomplished. We were occupying Madison Square Garden for five nights. Rather than civil disobedience, there would be packed audiences. Rather than marches, there would be loud applause. Rather than chants, there would be music.

"What good is anything without music," Sluggo would say to me years later. "And MUSE was *great* music."

Sluggo (and many others) have never given up the No Nukes battle, even as daily evidence on the dangers of climate change spawns rigorous debates on the merits of nuclear as clean energy. "Why have I stuck with it all these years?" Sluggo answered me several years ago with pride. "Because I'm too stupid and too stubborn to stop."

Sluggo's quixotic perseverance, the musicians' generous contribution of their time, Sam's leadership, Tom's dogged insistence on doing it right, Iris's precision, Howard's quiet balance, and David's strategic brilliance combined in the grist of MUSE. So many more personalities poured into the grain, clashing and grinding. We made many strategic and technical errors along the way, being an irregular fusion of activists, rock stars, producers, union labor, organic farmers, and Native Americans. Everything somehow, in some way, sifted together.

I stood there that morning and took in the full enormity of *NO NUKES* in ticking lights. Musicians were tuning up their instruments in sound studios throughout Manhattan. Concertgoers would be thinking about when to arrive. Stagehands could show up any moment to start the preparations. It was time for me to join this parade, however wrung out I was.

In the MUSE office, phones rang nonstop. I spoke to many reporters. There was constant interruption as I tried to gather together my many lists of party attendees, sponsors, VIPs, and others who would be admitted to mingle with the rock stars. Volunteers lugged boxes of programs and T-shirts to the Garden. Sluggo was finishing up a press release. David dashed in and out, not saying a word to anyone. I may have been the last one to leave the office, carefully locking the door.

Someone at Madison Square Garden handed me my full-access backstage pass, good for all five nights. I hung it around my neck on its lanyard and fingered the plastic coating. I could now go anywhere in this huge cavernous arena. As the seats filled, I paced through the endless rows and began memorizing each entryway to the backstage. I would not get lost.

Yet backstage nothing made sense, not even in rock and roll terms. Two antinuclear activists stood in the hallway discussing organizing tactics. Jackson Browne lured a beefy security guard away from his usual night of five-card draw to lecture him on the dangers of nuclear power. Graham Nash and John Hall spotted a visiting David Bowie and descended on him, but Bowie managed to escape without committing himself to the still-tentative lineup for the final night concert.

From the backstage wings, I heard the music start. Instruments magnified before me, my chest swelling to absorb everything. I didn't exhale until Bonnie Raitt finished commanding her band through a soulful rendition of "Angel from Montgomery." Then the Doobie Brothers filled the huge space with their percussion and vocals.

Musicians with full bands and roadies—enough people to fill 150 hotel rooms at six different hotels—paraded through the backstage area. When I went across the street to the Statler Hilton to get more program books as the first night wound down, everyone encountered was part of a band, a volunteer in a No Nukes T-shirt, a pubescent groupie with purple hair, or someone who listened from the rows on a $18.50 ticket and walked out still singing, lighting up another joint.

Grandiose thoughts kicked out my paranoia about not being able to send out money to the grassroots. MUSE truly had taken over Manhattan. No longer contained in a crowded office, I reveled in listening to the music, hearing the explosive applause, walking on the streets and soaring. Being slightly manic put me on par with everyone else.

At the opening night post-concert party, Crosby, Stills, and Nash could resume old relations and patch up more recent miscommunications. Whether Neil Young would show up for the fifth concert was still a question mark. An alarming number of tickets remained unsold for that last night. While not a messianic regrouping of the Beatles, the poignant Crosby, Stills, Nash, and Young would have resonance nearly a decade after their antiwar protest music had captured iconic moments, including the National Guardsmen shooting of four students on an Ohio college campus. My brother often listened to their music with his bedroom door shut, the soulful lyrics reaching me in my room across the hall where I lay trying to fall asleep.

Everyone was in great spirits that first night. At some point, Iris signaled for me to follow her into a backroom, where she laid out cocaine lines on a mirror. My mind already in hyper mode, I did not need the drug but enjoyed the clear rush. It would be the only lines I snorted during the run of the five concerts, yet the potent stimulant would not release its grip. I barely shut my eyes or ate anything through the marathon days that followed.

During the second-night concert, a slight mishap occurred. *Save the Planet,* the five-minute film produced for the concerts, didn't function. Technicians flooded the projector room. Film images again filled the backdrop. Then the huge mushrooming cloud of a nuclear test sputtered out. On the third try, the short film played through. The Green Mountain Post Films people had worked with Jayne and the Rafferty brothers to edit a strong montage of footage into a powerful punch. The audience responded with resounding cries of "No Nukes!"

Backstage, many SOS phone calls were getting made to secure a headline act for the fifth night. Graham Nash poked his head outside his dressing-room door and grabbed the first person walking by in a No Nukes T-shirt. "I've got John Lennon on the phone. He's in Algiers and he's interested in this concert and may be a part of it. Could you talk to him and convince him why nukes are so dangerous?"

Gil Scott-Heron took the stage. This very tall, handsome Black man surveyed the enormous crowd, and then his deep voice erupted with lyrics about almost losing Detroit.

The audience quieted down. Only the sound of joints being lit flickered throughout the huge arena. What might Karen Silkwood say to you if she was still alive? his song asked.

What would Karen have said tonight? These concerts were a small vindication for her death. Backstage, drinking wine, I imagined that I was speaking for Karen Silkwood as I wrangled our big donors—mostly young scions of old money—to give more. I watched musicians scurrying about, laughing, talking, hugging. They were wildly enthusiastic. I, too, remained elated.

Newspapers across the country, around the world, were writing articles about MUSE. My quotes showed up in the *Washington Post*, *New York Post*, *Rolling Stone*, and many other publications. Everyone everywhere knew we were occupying Madison Square Garden.

The third and fourth nights of the MUSE concerts were all about Bruce Springsteen, who was pacing backstage, nervous because he hadn't been on stage in over a year. The Boss transformed the moment he walked out, and the crowd went crazy. Young, impetuous, as in love with his audience as they were with him. It was as if no one else played those nights except for Springsteen. He turned thirty up there on the stage, hitting the high-octane mark of the concerts when performing "Thunder Road" with his acrobatic swagger, bouncing off backup horns, and sliding into perfect cheerleader splits on the same stage where Barnum and Bailey had let huge elephants unfurl equally loud instruments. He performed his full medley with the original E Street Band those two nights, displaying all the Jersey grit and genuine passion that would propel him into the mightiest echelon of rock performers.

I met Robert and Charlene for lunch on Saturday in the West Village, since I had their tickets for the MUSE Springsteen concert that night.

"You look wrung out, Susan," Robert said.

"I'm trying to control a concert marathon. There's no break," I snapped, then felt bad.

"Well, Susan," my brother began, "I am really proud of you. This is a big deal, and you pulled it off—"

"With many other people," I interrupted.

"But you were there at the start. I remember when you told me at the wedding. 'We're going to Madison Square Garden next.' I'd said, 'No way.' And here you are, doing it, my little sister."

"How's everything in Baltimore?" I asked, but my mind had already drifted.

Growing up, nearly everyone—parents, family, friends, teachers—expected Robert would be the one to conquer the world. Yet, instead, the quiet wisp of a girl, the one everyone ignored, had aimed for the stars. I should take some joy in this. But I didn't. If I could truly reach high enough to grab the brass ring, I would hand that marvel to my brother. "Be whatever you want," I'd say.

I joined Iris late that night in a limousine to pick up Jesse Colin Young at JFK, drinking champagne out of crystal flutes included in the car's rich interior. Tim Sexton had sent us on this errand; the journey provided the break we needed to reinforce ourselves for getting through one last day of MUSE.

As the driver took us toward the airport, Iris told me how disillusioning the MUSE experience had become for her. "People hiding behind *the cause* to make excuses for being rude and demanding." And, with MUSE time running out, the tasks had become more onerous. We were not dreaming up ways to shut down nukes. We were trying to avert production crises. We were both crashing from the crazy elation of those first few nights of concerts.

"I can't even think straight," I confessed.

Iris laughed. "You never did think straight. That's why we love you."

I wanted to tell her I was scared, but only admitted, "I haven't slept, barely eaten, and sometimes I'm not sure if what I'm seeing is really happening."

She took my hands and wove our fingers together. "Hey, I'm here. I'm seeing all this, too. I promise you this is all really happening."

Iris could always ground me, or at least give me the semblance of normalcy, a relative term with the two of us. After all, I was the only candidate for the *Rolling Stone* job who didn't walk into her office and rattle off rock-and-roll trivia. I came in and talked about everything but music. I reminded her of our first meeting as the limousine raced through the streets of Queens.

"You were off the wall. The only job applicant who didn't make *me* feel crazy."

"I was crazy."

"That's why I hired you."

We laughed and tightened our hold on each other.

How I wish I had never let go of Iris. Or, as with Robert, that I could have seen through the facade. Every time she disappeared around the revolving tube into the production dark room at *Rolling Stone*, I merely assumed she needed a break. I never understood the depth of her destructive drug dependency. Somehow, after the concerts, after everything faded, after I had moved to Washington, Iris drifted further and further off. No one from *Rolling Stone* or MUSE had talked to her for years when we learned that Iris had succumbed to drugs. But that night, as MUSE was winding down, I only saw her as a kindred spirit and somewhat magical.

CHAPTER 29

Life throws us opportunities. We're forced to make choices. Robert Frost says it best in "The Road Not Taken" when he poignantly sets off his poem with a description of diverging roads in a yellow wood. My brother confronted such divergent roads when he returned to the Apollo shirt factory after having taken a solid job with another clothing manufacturer. The move was a disaster; then, roads diverged again. This time our father offered to launch him in business. How could Robert refuse the capital that would allow him to open his own shirt-manufacturing factory? We cheered him on. No one factored in how very complicated his relationship was with Dad.

In New York City, with far less at stake, I once tangoed with seductive danger when roads diverged.

I shall be telling this with a sigh
Somewhere ages and ages hence

During my first year at *Rolling Stone*, I very much wanted to be initiated into the grimiest spot in New York City, a mecca for rebellious punkers from every borough.

"I am city savvy," I'd told Susanne, another *Rolling Stone* staffer. Leveraging one of my favorite words, I said, "I can be dissident." Nothing could jolt me, even CBGBs. Derived from country, bluegrass, and blues, CBGBs was an infamous venue of punk rock and new wave.

Susanne, who came from the music industry, and her boyfriend Tom, soon to be a founder of MTV, finally agreed to accompany me to the stripped-down music joint with no delusions of grandeur. It meant a trip down to the Bowery in the city's eastside wasteland and being repeatedly warned on what to avoid. Eat nothing. Touch nothing. Step carefully.

With so much anticipation, I was still surprised to find the place such a dive. Bare floors, no decor except a few dark posters, a makeshift stage that barely removed the music from the audience, the smell of yesterday's beer, and a retinue of punk characters crowded into a space about the size of a college classroom. But also explosions of metallic flashes from the stage lighting and the promise of the Ramones, who I had never heard, or heard of, prior to moving to Manhattan.

I took care to bone up on the group. It had been a year since the release of their first album, *Ramones,* which music critic Paul Nelson described as "constructed almost entirely of rhythm tracks of an exhilarating intensity rock and roll has not experienced since its earliest days." Despite only limited commercial success, these unrelated musicians, all using the last name Ramone, indelibly marked the fledgling punk movement.

We arrived at CBGBs to long lines of punkers wrapped around city blocks of darkened buildings and filling the void with incongruous streaks of purple. Escorted by Susanne and Tom, I felt squeezed and oddly silenced bypassing the hoard and moving straight through to the very front of the line. Tom ensured the doors would open for us. We showed our *Rolling Stone* press passes.

Inside CBGBs the crowd seemed to belong. We walked into the center of their vortex. The vibrations were so tremendous I felt them massaging my feet and sending shimmers up my legs.

My new red leather shoes turned black as we slogged through spilled beer and Clorox. One of the sound technicians winked at me, and I winked back. I imagined his eyes following me and turned around to smile. He rewarded me with a sly beckoning look. The crowd yanked me away, and my escorts steered me to a reserved table before the stampede began.

The boys from Queens tore into their music, pounding out simple lyrics in two-minute bites. Surf city crashing onto a graffiti shore. The persistent drumming shook the room with a tempo that never changed. Joey, Johnny, Dee Dee, and Tommy took over the room. All the Ramones moved their bony hips with the tempo, in torn jeans and rubber-soled shoes, electric guitars played from the groin. I couldn't quite hear the words, just the constant repetitions. No whining solos. Just hammering, constant and energetic. Many people danced, some wriggled and writhed, and others leaped into the air while the band kept the amplifiers on high. We remained seated and still. Then the set ended potent and clear, like a martini neat.

Someone put Mink DeVille on the turntable and the record played far quieter than the live act. I could think again. Lighting flooded the room, transforming silhouettes and shadows into people. I couldn't see the sexy sound technician, though I looked. Relaxing, I rolled some Drum tobacco in cigarette paper and asked the waitress for my new favorite drink.

"No," Susanne and Tom firmly stated in unison. They waved away the waitress and I was startled to learn that I'd just committed a colossal *faux pas* by asking for an Irish coffee.

Susanne leaned over and whispered, "You can't drink anything here that doesn't come in a closed bottle. The guys who work here piss everywhere. And they never wash out anything."

Tom, ever the gentleman, bought us three Budweisers from the bar. The bottled beer was warm, tasteless, and safe. I felt suitably chastised for thinking I knew what to do in the punk world.

There would be no Random Note to grab that night for the magazine column. The Ramones left so quickly after their concluding act ended that I could nearly hear them running down the street. I had missed something. I was there in the Bowery, but I wasn't there at all. Something shielded me from truly embracing the culture of such boldly un-American antiauthoritarian music. It was brazen and I, merely a marshmallow asking for Irish coffee.

Tom led us out of CBGBs. I wanted to yank away from Tom's courtly hand on my arm and run back into the club, find the sound technician who had winked at me earlier in the evening; stay and be bold.

I could hear the next act tuning up. At CBGBs, endless experimental bands were always waiting for the opportunity to jam. The dyed-hair, wild-eyed fans never left until splatches of daylight broke the sky. I would go back in. Rather than being straight-jacketed by Susanne and Tom, I'd venture forth alone and dance wildly, catching words flung back and forth among the initiated to stuff in my reporter's notebook, words to write up later. I would flex the dissidence in me. I would become initiated.

My escorts paced ahead. Hearing something like a cold wind whistling, I turned. Inside CBGBs beckoned with its rambunctious grind and permeating yeasty odor. Outside, the city was quieting with streets nearly empty. Above, street lights blinded me. I thought of the wink, the smile, the unknown possibilities waiting for me inside.

I stopped, unsure which road to take. Music lifted me and I floated back toward the beckoning sounds, flashes, gyrations of limbs.

I heard a voice. "Hurry Susan." Tom helped me into the taxi.
Next time, I thought.

Yet knowing how way leads on to way
I doubted if I should ever come back.

I never returned to CBGBs. My moment to venture into the
center of that vortex had passed. My dissident passions were
eventually funneled along a very different road. Had I turned back,
though, it is possible I would have experienced the scene with more
immediacy, gathered material to write something good, spoken with
the sound technician.

Or, alone in the Bowery so very late, I might have only
encountered danger.

Robert took the more trodden road and accepted the parental
bestowal to open his own shirt factory. Did he know, I wonder, that
he had segued onto a dangerous path? Had I been walking with my
brother in the woods, knowing more, I might have urged him on the
less-traveled road—one less fraught with risks.

CHAPTER 30

The last day of MUSE started very early. We had the limousine take Jesse Colin Young directly to the Battery Park City No Nukes rally, where brigades of volunteers were finishing the risers and roping off the VIP areas. My job, since I could identify the entourages, was to ensure that only sanctioned people were allowed beyond the ropes, away from the two hundred thousand spectators who would gather in reverie and protest in the dayglow of that Sunday morning.

Battery Park City became everything that Don Ross and Pam Lippe had hoped for as they organized their second large rally that year with a strong activist coalition behind them—first the May 6 rally in Washington, DC and now this one on September 23. Three Mile Island had nearly melted down less than six months earlier. "No Nukes! No Nukes! No Nukes!" People chanted as if the whole world could hear. And they did hear. People hoisted banners proclaiming, *Nuclear Power Kills*. Others asked, *Did Karen Silkwood die for nothing?*

Sunshine drowned the dusty spit of land on the Hudson River in a gentle late September light. Music that had clamored for days on electric overdrive in Madison Square Garden simmered acoustically against the river into a lulling medley. High on the risers, above the crowd, John Trudell lifted his arms toward the sky in full Native headdress and gear. He appeared to be praying to the heavens. Large film cameras followed the American Indian Movement activist as he paced the stage. With Warner Brothers involved in the *No Nukes* movie, our low-budget feature documentary had ballooned into a full-scale production.

The rally aligned the music and the politics, pounding lower Manhattan with a sense of togetherness as latecomer Graham Nash swung by with a "Cheerio" to collect his badge, though everyone knew the British singer-songwriter. Lingering near the front gate, caught in the lens of photographer Peter Simon, Graham leaned over to graze cheeks with Peter's wife, Ronni, in warm greeting before striding over to the risers. "What a day," he said, from over his shoulder, eyes sparkling.

Tom Hayden led his wife Jane Fonda through the entry point. They didn't wait for passes and no one stopped them. Tom acknowledged me with a wave. He wanted the hundreds of names and addresses that I had in my files, the hard core of the antinuclear movement, for his upcoming multiple-city political tour with Jane. But he wouldn't get them from me. Those in-depth files on activists across the country that I had spent weeks sorting through, and carefully evaluating, would eventually be safely archived with many other papers from that period at the University of Massachusetts-Amherst.

Later that day, the fifth and last concert with a much smaller audience than the prior ones whizzed by as I burrowed ever deeper into a gauzy mix of sound, crowds, and exhaustion—teetering closer and closer to the edge.

Someone whispered to me that fugitive antiwar activist Abbie Hoffman had infiltrated MUSE. "You know him."

"No I don't."

"Sure you do."

Man, I was just a kid in '68 when Abbie turned the Democratic Convention in Chicago into Guerilla Theater. In '79, he was facing dope charges and running underground from the Feds. Surely, I couldn't know this fugitive—*know him*, that is, unless under an alias.

As the music continued, little Abbies began to pop out of my brain's corn-mush as curly-haired raisins. I tried to match his face, or what I remembered of his face from photographs, against all the people crowding the backstage around me. With plastic surgery, he could be anyone. I glanced suspiciously into the features of my coorganizers. Does anyone else know a fugitive is among us? Is it a conspiracy?

I was crashing. But before plunging, I came to a sudden realization in a burst of refracted light off dangling disco balls during the after-party at Les Mouches. *I know the fugitive Abbie Hoffman.* Of course! He's Barry Freed, the funny dark-haired Save the River guy who hangs out at the office and gives everyone T-shirts. His nose and chin had totally been altered, but those piercing eyes, black darts, were a dead giveaway. I'd given him a desk. I had harbored a fugitive at MUSE.

Someone tried to dance with me, and I whirled and whirled and whirled. I was lost again, not sure how I got to the very center of the dance floor. Unable to recognize anyone in that psychedelic lighting contorting into purple, green, and red searchlights, I became convinced the Feds were after me.

It would be better not to let anyone know. My secret. Maybe the Feds would not think to check the MUSE office. Even so, I decided to plant his T-shirts in another location to put them off his scent.

As I wandered through the crowded nightclub rooms, many people grabbed me, thanking me for all I had done. Bonnie Raitt hugged me for a long time. Some people were speculating what might come next: more big concerts, a MUSE West. *"Don't you know,"* I tried to say, "We might not have much money to give away. We might not have anything." Either I never got those words out or no one could hear what I said. Everyone kept smiling at me, and the noise was deafening.

Before I left that night, Sam handed me an envelope: a large check from Madison Square Garden, five nights of ticket sales. "Get it to our officer at the bank first thing in the morning. Can you do that?"

"Yeah, sure." As treasurer of the MUSE Foundation, I was the keeper of our bank account. They knew me there when I showed up a few hours later, and the officer who oversaw our account was happy to deposit the check. Except, because the check was for well over a million dollars, the nice officer suggested I put the cash in a short-term certificate of deposit.

"You did what?" Sam said later, trying to remain calm. And he quietly explained that the money was not really ours. That bundle of cash would have to pay for all the hotel rooms and other expenses that had accumulated over the past weeks. We had not made money on the concerts. Our only hope was to recoup everything and much more off the record album set and feature film.

When I walked back out on the street after canceling the brief investment, the craggy, altered face of Barry Freed zapped into view. He flickered then vanished, laughing hysterically. Again and again, I heard Abbie's high-pitched laugh, loud, because everything about him rattled societal barriers. He was a fugitive, which gave me no choice.

I had to get out of New York City, and the fastest escape was to Harrisburg. The train from Penn Station got me through the Jersey flats and into the farm country of Pennsylvania. I rested my head against the window and stared out at the rolling scenery, whishing by fast enough to give me a sense of getting away. Out of New York, I felt safer. Then somehow my mind focused on Jack Kerouac and the night he had spent at the Harrisburg bus/train station in his odyssey, *On the Road*. Something about that station was suspect, but I couldn't remember what.

What if the Feds are waiting for me at the Harrisburg station? I panicked and walked between cars of the train, feeling I was headed into trouble and not out of it. The Feds must know I'd harbored Abbie Hoffman. But it was too late to go back, too late to reverse the last months of my life. The forward motion of the train slowly joggled me back to my seat. I didn't move again until the conductor announced Harrisburg.

The big car was waiting, engine still on. But the Feds would never allow a drooling oversized poodle in the backseat. Andy stuck out his droopy head and shook his mangled curls with excitement.

"Get in," Dad yelled.

My father knew immediately I was as burnt and useless as charred barnyard timber. He didn't ask me any questions. Shirley kept the television on with old movies playing and wrapped me in a warm blanket.

I could hear them whispering. "She will be all right," Shirley said. "She's just exhausted."

"I've never seen her this bad."

How bad am I? I wondered.

As they slept, I tried to clear my mind. But visions of the past week wouldn't leave me—flashing lights, crowds, music, crashing. *Why can't I turn it off?* I put pillows over my head, smothering my face in one. But I couldn't shut everything out.

I stayed in bed until I heard Dad and Shirley heading to work. Their car engines sounded like shotguns.

Then quiet set in. Stillness so pure I could hear rumbling inside my head. *The concerts are over. Done. You have to get up. You have to run. You can't make things all right again. People will find you. Leave now.*

I walked fast across the fields to the fast-running creek that had always been a refuge for me. Lying flat on my back, I stared at the sky and the tops of the trees with leaves just barely tinged by autumn's nearness.

As I waited to fall over the edge, Robert found me.

CHAPTER 31

Justin Ross Kellam wailed. In the few heartbeats it took for the mohel to perform my godson's circumcision, I considered that one day I might have a family. But there was something I had to do first.

The months after the MUSE concerts were rough.

We would not hit the million-dollar goal, not even close. Some would say that the shrunken bundle of cash from the concerts and its offshoots was of little consequence considering the magnitude of publicity the events generated. Timing was everything. Public sentiment toward nuclear power soured in the wake of Three Mile Island and nearly all orders for new US reactors, many under construction, would be canceled in the late seventies and eighties.

We kept the MUSE office open after the concerts and the foundation board went through all the motions of deciding where the money would go, though we had nothing in the bank. I spent weeks preparing summaries of the proposals and organizing the requests for grants by geographic region. When the three-record MUSE album set came out before Christmas and went gold, we were hopeful there might be cash to distribute.

No Nukes the movie opened in New York City on July 19, 1980 to mild acclaim. I viewed the film from a comfortable seat at a Cinema I theater, able to relax and enjoy moments like Bruce Springsteen's rendition of "Thunder Road" when he leaps all over the stage and then feigns a collapse. "I can't go on like this! I'm thirty years old! My heart is startin' to go!" His band, looking concerned, coaxes him up on the count. A moment of quiet, and then the Boss leaps up and starts in on "Quarter to Three," and the live concert audience roars.

When early moviegoers didn't fill theaters, however, Warner Brothers yanked *No Nukes* from theatrical distribution. That fast. Gone, despite all the big names and megabucks we'd thrown into this venture. For all the artistry and political commitment of the concerts, the brilliance of its communications' reach, and the precedent it set for many megaconcert benefits that followed, MUSE gambled and lost in Hollywood.

Disconcerting facts came to light: the film had gone $200,000 over budget, and the money we were anticipating from Elektra/ Asylum on record sales came instead as a loan through Warner Brothers. Our profits from the album set had subsidized a movie that lost everything. Despite it all, we did manage to send out roughly a quarter-million dollars in grants to the grassroots movement.

I slowly accepted that it was time to move on with my life. Though I recouped from my quasi-breakdown, the eggshell of vulnerability clung. Loud noises rattled me, and Manhattan closed in. I turned twenty-seven when we made the collective decision to put MUSE on hold as 1980 ended. Ronald Reagan would soon be entering the White House and a disgruntled young man had taken the life of John Lennon.

Only Justin's birth in January 1981 signified hope.

When Charlene was upstairs putting Justin to sleep with the

warmth of her milk and a lullaby tape softening the quiet, Robert, though tired, fixed his penetrating gaze on me for the first time that day. "Something is going on with you." Said as fact.

I sighed, sunk deeper into his living room sofa. "This is the year."

"For what?"

"Becoming a writer."

"You've always written," Robert said while stepping into the kitchen. "What's different now?" He pulled a can of ginger ale from the refrigerator and offered me one.

I shook my head. "Writing is something I've squeezed in between everything else: work, life, whatnot." Knitting my fingers behind my head, I paused a moment before continuing. "I have to find out if it's something I can really do. You know, see if I have what it takes to write the great American novel."

Robert didn't laugh. "Well, then, go for it."

That summer I rented the annex to Crosby Lodge, an elegant nineteenth-century shingled home on the shores of Frenchman's Bay at one of Maine's numerous picturesque points and drove up in late June with little more than the Royal typewriter that had replaced my Olivetti. I set up my writing space on a screened-in alcove off my bedroom on the second floor. Nothing to block me but a panoramic view of coast, pine trees, and sailboats. I started every morning at sunbreak by typing a long letter to one of my friends back in New York. There was no telephone at Crosby Lodge. I was deliciously cut off from life.

In Maine, I could finally unravel from the demise of MUSE. I bought a bike and rode for miles and miles along the empty coastline. And I did write my novel, a perfectly terrible fictional account of what I had experienced during my New York City years. After five months, I packed those pages up in a cardboard box and decided it was time to become a journalist, eventually moving to Washington, DC.

CHAPTER 32

My father's offer to back Robert in a shirt manufacturing business was readily accepted. Dad had the capital to invest and believed his son would be able to handle the pressures of running his own factory. Unemployed after being shoved out of our uncle's rapidly condensing Apollo shirt factory, Robert, with a wife and two children to support after Jenna's birth in 1983, badly needed the work. In ordinary circumstances, Robert might have done very well. He had considerable experience in many aspects of the shirt business. But he had several things going against him. Throughout the 1980s, much US manufacturing fled to shores where labor was cheap, which quickly rendered Robert's product noncompetitive.

Something else happened. Something deeply tucked inside Robert surfaced. His relationship with our father had been poisoned long ago and toxicity remained. Hard as I tried, I could not pry out what was actually occurring in the murky unfolding of events.

Robert wound up in the hospital with blood in his urine, and the doctors traced the problem to Coumadin, a blood thinner also used to poison rats. Public health officials thoroughly combed his factory in Dundalk just outside the city of Baltimore and found nothing. Therapists in the hospital drilled Robert to ensure the poison was not self-ingested. They concluded it was not and discharged him.

I bought tickets to take Justin and Jenna to the Russian Circus at the Baltimore Civic Center soon after to give my brother a quiet afternoon to relax and recuperate with his wife. A public health doctor, Tom, joined me. More a good friend than a romantic partner, Tom's being an officer with the US Public Health Service proved invaluable. With his knowledge of poisons as occupational workplace hazards, Tom explained how people could be exposed to warfarin, the active ingredient in Coumadin, by breathing it in, swallowing it, skin absorption, and even eye contact. Yet, it remained a conundrum how Robert could unknowingly, and repeatedly, come in contact with the poison. Then the lingering question: why were none of the factory workers affected?

I was anxious for Tom to meet my brother. We drove to the small house in the Baltimore subdivision to pick up my niece and nephew, intentionally arriving early. Robert's still form was visible in the large living room window as we approached the front door. Even through the plate glass, I detected listlessness in the slouch of his body and the way he stared straight ahead, not focusing on anything in particular.

Charlene let us in. Justin bounded down the steps two at a time. "Dancing bears," he yelled. He leaped three times before giving me a special "bear hug."

"Save all that energy for the circus," Robert chided. I watched the light rekindle in my brother's eyes as he gazed at his son.

My niece, Jenna, dressed sweetly in a fluffy jumper only appeared to be more dignified. She could be as unruly as her brother, even delighted in egging him on, but knew how to temper her demeanor when necessary. She politely shook Tom's extended hand.

Giving my brother and Tom an opportunity to interact, I went over afternoon logistics with Charlene.

"No cotton candy," she said.

Jenna gave me a knowing look. I was the infamous pushover aunt. Justin, ever in motion, only wanted to get going. There was something so very special about going to a Russian circus for an eight-year-old, something furiously exotic and wondrously fun.

Only after a full afternoon of Russian pageantry, the much-ballyhooed dancing bears, hilarity, amazing human feats of athleticism, and more than enough sugary treats to appease my young charges, did we return the exhausted kids to their parents and head back to Washington.

"What did you think?" I couldn't wait to ask Tom that question.

As he drove, eyes on the road, his lips pursed, and his fingers tightened on the wheel. "Tough, really tough to say."

What had he seen? I prodded.

"Logic would suggest he knew about the poison."

"But?"

"Your brother has all the appearances of a contented man. I didn't sense any danger signs."

As we whipped down I-95, Tom admitted he was flummoxed. "I could get another team of people to go through his factory. But I don't think they'll find anything."

Such searches seldom uncovered the real problem, he explained, his voice trying unsuccessfully to soothe. My broken fingernails dug into my palms and drew blood, but I didn't feel the pain, only a deep sadness for the limits of my ability to unearth the right clues.

◆　◆　◆

After some difficulties at the factory, Dad put another two hundred grand into Robert's business, and everything appeared to be going well. Only a guise, we learned too late.

The second time Robert went into the hospital, his close friend Sandy, a urologist, began to question Robert. "I don't get it," Sandy told me over the phone. "I can't figure out how he's ingesting the rat poison. He swears it's not him. And it certainly isn't Charlene."

The computer keyboard on my desk at work began wavering. I couldn't focus my eyes or my thoughts. What if he is doing this to himself?

"I'm coming to see you," I yelled into the phone to my brother, trying to be heard above the clattering noise in the medical ward. "Can I bring you anything?"

"Hey, yeah, pick up an Italian sub, with everything."

"Even hot peppers."

"Especially hot peppers."

I saw Robert the moment the elevator doors opened. He was walking away, his hospital gown flapping, his hands pulling a mobile stand hung with a bladder of fluid being fed into his veins. That indelible image is with me still. My brother had always cast an aura of strength, invincibility, and health. Seeing him connected by plastic tubing to the intravenous apparatus revealed a vulnerability I had never allowed myself to associate with him. I called his name; he turned, all smiles and delight at seeing me.

Had what I'd seen only moments before been a mirage? Or, was his sunny greeting the work of a practiced actor?

"You remembered the sub."

"With hot peppers." I handed him the bag. Rather than devouring the nonhospital food, he led me on a short walk to a small kitchen. I couldn't help but see the refrigerator shelves lined with identical paper-wrapped Italian subs.

"Are those all yours?"

Robert nodded, not at all embarrassed by having asked every

visitor to bring him exactly the same sandwich. As he was slowly withdrawing from family and friends, he could only voice the simplest of requests. He probably was pleading for real help. Sounding an alarm. But all that came out was a simple ask for a heavily loaded sandwich he would never eat.

Robert was to be discharged the very next day, he told me. Being Halloween, my brother was anxious to get out of the hospital to take the children trick-or-treating. Even weak, he again managed to break through all the hurdles and be released from the hospital.

I did not know what to ask my brother that could penetrate the sudden steeliness of his eyes. He swore to me, and to everyone else, that he didn't know how the poison had entered his bloodstream. Scores of public health experts thoroughly checked everywhere Robert had been and found nothing. The psychiatric team that spoke with him at the hospital remained firmly convinced he had not taken the poison intentionally. Two realities were going on simultaneously, and I couldn't grasp both.

CHAPTER 33

For some years after Robert's death, a recurrent dream of him being alive, but seriously ill, haunted my sleep. I was caring for him in a vague gauze-draped world that seemed to exclude everyone else. He would be lying in the bed we had shared long ago in the house that Grandpa Abe built, and I stayed by my brother in that room, taking care of his every need. The forsythia bushes bloomed on spidery yellow stalks, even as ice designs spread on the windows. Everything was seen only from the inside looking out. Robert had become my entire world. I dedicated myself to him totally.

I would wake up sad, spooked; maybe too, a tad relieved. There was also the guilt. Why was I able to proceed with my own life when I couldn't save his?

If only I had not been so self-centered, so concerned with myself, so unable to put his interests above my own, he might have lived.

Several things occurred toward the end of his life; how I handled them, how badly, tore at me.

One of those incidents had seemed insignificant at the time, barely more than a test of wills. But after his death, I saw the chain of events differently. Robert had inadvertently left his eyeglasses at a client's, someone he was helping at night with a computer system. He was moonlighting to bring in more money. Robert asked me to drive to his client's house off the Washington Beltway in Maryland to retrieve the left-behind item after I finished work in Virginia, many miles away.

"Do you know what the Washington Beltway is like at rush hour?"

I heard his steady breathing through the phone. "You don't have to do it today. Maybe tomorrow?"

"You don't have a back-up pair?"

"No."

"Robert, I really wish I could help you. But asking me to get on and off the parking-lot ramps of the Washington Beltway at that hour is more than I can do."

I thought the matter resolved, until I saw my dad some weeks later and he reamed me out for being selfish. "You should have picked up his glasses. He doesn't ask much of you."

Tears prickled my eyes. My defense was ebbing away. "You don't know how hard it is to fight traffic on the Beltway. It would have taken me hours."

"Your brother asked you to do it."

It was that simple. Robert had asked me to do something that I perceived as an inconvenience. How difficult would it have been to take a few hours out of my day to help my brother? Everything during that last year of his life became embossed in stark relief. I did not take the time to tackle Beltway traffic, but I have had far too much time since to replay and try to understand why I refused him.

I also wrestle with things that happened during what would become his last Thanksgiving. My rent-controlled Georgetown house proved wonderful for entertaining, with its large living room overlooking Volta Park and a cavernous dining area with a fireplace on the first floor. Let me cook the turkey this year, I told Robert and my mother months earlier. The second Coumadin incident still fresh, I wanted the holidays to be special. My brother agreed to drive to Washington, even after an early snowstorm hit and slickened the roads on Thanksgiving morning. Although Robert was willing to travel, some of my neighbors opted to stay put; of course, I invited them over. A turkey meal can be expansive, and that was the way I was feeling when I awoke to the lovely blanket of snow. Rodrigo, his friends Isobel and Hall with their young child, all of whom spoke perfect French, would arrive as Europeans often do, when they were ready.

Robert drove the Baltimore family in early. He settled on my living room sofa, comfortably watching football, as Justin and Jenna ran my dog, Ouija, up and down the winding steps and the rest of us gathered in the kitchen to prepare the meal. My mother and Charlene were both expert help at everything culinary. It might have been a very cozy Thanksgiving. Already, the smell of roasting turkey had spread to all three floors of my townhouse.

"Hello. Hello." Isobel walked through the door with bottles of wine and an air of festivity that always trailed her like chiffon. Rodrigo followed with kisses for everyone, as he had already met my family during a Rosh Hashana lunch in Baltimore. A handsome Chilean doctor, Rodrigo upped the voltage on Isobel's charm. The professorial Hall came later with the child.

I asked Robert to turn off the football game. He did so, but I can still see, in my memory of his vacant eyes, the shot of pain I inflicted by allowing my foreign-born neighbors to invade and dominate our low-key American tradition. Football has always been a crucial part of Thanksgiving. Yet, instead, I allowed the loquacious Rodrigo and Isobel to domineer my living room.

Robert might have asked to keep the game on, perhaps offered to lower the volume. A younger, stronger Robert could easily have prevailed. But the Robert I knew had already started to fade.

The last time I saw my brother was Mother's Day, 1990.

A relationship conundrum with my AP reporter boyfriend, Dick, weighed on my mind as I drove from Georgetown to Baltimore that Sunday. We were at that pivotal point of weighing whether or not to keep the romance going. With my own muddle, I couldn't see how withdrawn Robert had become as we sat down to grilled hot dogs and hamburgers, Justin and Jenna running amok. My mother, in fine spirits with all her kids around her, held up her wine glass to make a toast. She had never warmed up fully to Charlene but had the grace to pretend. "I want to thank my lovely daughter-in-law for giving me these wonderful grandchildren."

We all knew it might be years, if ever, before I could do the same. As a good aunt, though, I brought the kids swag from a recent assignment covering the launch of the Hubble Space Telescope. Justin, at eight, proudly displayed all the colorful NASA pins and Hubble posters. Six-year-old Jenna immediately ripped the cellophane wrapping from her chocolate Hubble and stuck the top of the candy space telescope in her mouth.

"Save some of that," Charlene warned her daughter. But Jenna would always have a mind of her own.

I talked to Robert about Dick when we managed to be alone. My brother had settled on a large armchair that day and barely got up. Sitting beside him in a folding chair, I told him that I wasn't sure whether Dick, seven years younger than me, was ready to settle down.

"He'd be lucky to have you."

I squeezed Robert's hand. "You don't like that I'm still alone."

"I worship the ground my kids walk on. Of course I want you to have a family too."

"And yes," he added. "I don't want you to be alone."

An hour or so later, as I prepared to drive to Dick's apartment on Capitol Hill, Robert stood up, asking, "Why do you have to leave so soon? Stay longer."

I could have, but I didn't. Robert hugged me tight for what seemed like many minutes. Did my brother know then that he would never see me again?

CHAPTER 34

Robert gave up life on his twelfth wedding anniversary. I can only think he chose that day rather than celebrate a marriage and a family to which he no longer felt worthy. He had run his business and Dad's investment into the ground. Taking risks, being irresponsible with money, he seemed to have followed a semiconscious path to repeat the sins of the father. No longer thinking rationally, he allowed the buried past to rush out and swamp him. He succumbed to that noxious ache he had locked behind an impeccable lifetime performance.

He tricked us. Everyone believed him when he said he had no idea how he'd consumed the rat poison. That flirting with destruction had been a cry for help, but none of us could penetrate through to the truth. He refused to allow us.

Had Robert planned to depart from us on his twelfth wedding

anniversary? No one knows what goes on inside a marriage. I have always suspected Robert married Charlene, besides her beauty and kindness, for her inability to wrangle inside another person's psyche. I knew that about her early on. She largely takes things as they come.

When dissecting those final months, I often question why Charlene did not pick up on his slow withdrawal. How could she not sense—in the man she laid beside every night—the roiling pain that finally pushed him, consciously or not, to take the car keys that Monday morning as their anniversary approached and forever vanish from our lives?

I have to remind myself that my sister-in-law is a smart cookie, no one's fool. Robert's brilliant disguise was just too good.

Robert was on the road for many hours on June 4, having left his house very early in the morning but not reaching his factory—where he chose to end his life—until long after the work day ended, and everyone was gone. Although it was a warm, sunny day, his retrieved car revealed he had the heat turned up high. Was he already shutting down and consequently chilled? Knowing Dad and Shirley were traveling, and that my father kept a gun, he might have driven as far as Harrisburg. Not thinking clearly, he might not have considered the house security system. If he ever knew the code to get in, he perhaps forgot it that day. We later learned there were indications of attempts to crack the alarm system.

Where Robert traveled that day is pure speculation. He could have circled the Baltimore Beltway for hours, pacing off distance and how much farther he had left. Twelve years of marriage, such a milestone looming ahead.

Someone at the factory notified Charlene early in the day that Robert had not arrived at work. Attempts were made to reach people, anyone who might know of Robert's whereabouts. My brother, especially as a husband and father, was never erratic. Declared officially missing, the police came to the house. My Aunt Shifra spent the night with my mother, though neither slept. Too much to take in, my mother's missing child.

Where was I? Downing shots of tequila with two AP reporters, I became ever more oblivious, unreachable, lost in a bar booth on Capitol Hill—miles from Robert.

◆   ◆   ◆

Afterward, I stayed for a long time in Baltimore, through the funeral and through many long days of sitting shiva. I stayed in his room, in his bed with Charlene. She couldn't be alone, and together we watched late-night television and talked.

"He was the love of my life," she told me then and tells me now.

"Did you see anything? Any signs?"

"Nothing," she has always insisted. "My marriage was great."

I wanted to believe the marriage was very good and provided some comfort to him as his grip on life slipped. The children were his greatest joy. Only overwhelming agony could break those precious bonds.

Slowly, as the days passed, people stopped arriving to pay their respects. Jenna kept a journal in her childish scrawl. She wrote with curiosity about why so many people were in her house. Days later, she asked in her large handwriting where they had all gone. Justin looked out the window one morning and asked, "Who will cut the grass now?"

As time went on, I visited my mother in Baltimore often, wanting to help her, but she stayed wrapped too tight. She would never accept my concept of grief: that one should openly mourn the loss, share vignettes of that person. After the initial weeks, she could hardly talk about Robert.

My father also had a very hard time grasping the finality of his son's act. "I'd just given him two hundred grand," he would say. "Sunk the money into that godforsaken business. And I would do it again. And again. Just to have more days with Robert."

Dad and Shirley would often join me on excursions with Justin and Jenna, a focal point, a living slice of Robert, a way to grieve through two precious receptacles of love. With Robert's children, we would go places like Chuck E. Cheese, with loud video games and pizza. Easily amused, their youthful exuberance lifted us.

My mother spent regular weekly time with Justin and Jenna as they grew up. She bought them books on report card days, and often guided them in table manners and politics. She insisted her grandchildren have a good grasp of current events.

For me, accepting the loss of my brother was an excruciating process. I found that grief starts on rocky shoals, as one must navigate barnacles and slippery rocks after the death. Then the tide comes in, serene shock as waves crest, nearly an absence of any feeling. The receding tide leaves residue, memories layered upon memories. Such a pattern of tides sweeping in and out went on for days, weeks. When the storm hit, the surface churned suddenly into unnavigable currents, irrational and dangerous.

Dick committed to our relationship and moved into my Georgetown townhouse. Grandson of a Northern Baptist minister, he knew what to say to keep me whole. There for me every night, we somehow made it through those summer months in 1990, through the steady motion of the tides. Everything changed when I could no longer navigate my emotions. Uncontrollable tears erupted and I tried to push Dick away. My erratic, irresponsible behavior forced my bosses at a Washington magazine to fire me.

I had read enough books on grief to know that this reactionary phase would occur. For weeks, my life spun faster and faster out of control. Nothing prepared me for my speeding bursts of rage, for how I could destroy a job, puncture a relationship, and lose my bearings.

Eventually, the tempest eased. Dick did not leave me. After a lengthy interview process, *Congressional Quarterly* hired me. I was only troubled by the continuation of my wild mood swings, still swerving dangerously nearly ten months after Robert's death. I felt nauseous and dizzy.

Someone suggested I might be pregnant.

It took me several weeks to get up the guts to buy a pregnancy test kit at the drugstore. Out running on the towpath along the C&O Canal on a Saturday morning, I swung by for the purchase on my way back. I sat alone in my kitchen and waited, feeding my dog Ouija my breakfast. The positive sign could not have been bolder. Rather than being crazy, I was with child.

I had survived the grief.

CHAPTER 35

I delivered a healthy nine-pound boy on December 20, 1991, a year and a half after losing Robert. Dick stood by me in the operating room as the doctors performed an emergency C-section after twenty-four hours of labor. Even heavily sedated with a copious mix of morphine and other heavy pain medication, I heard the raucous laughter of my obstetrician. "No wonder we had to go in and get him out," he told the assisting doctor. "This kid's nearly four years old already."

The first time I held the very long, round, robust Reid and looked into his milky brown eyes that already resembled mine, I silently wished for him to have my strength. Only ironclad willpower had propelled me forward for months, after losing my brother; again, after Dick moved out during the pregnancy.

Being the father, Dick had his rights and suitably asked for a say in how to proceed with the unexpected news. He'd asked me to consider an abortion.

"I can't."

We were sitting in the kitchen on a gorgeous spring day. Though sunlight never entered that dungeon-like room, we had opened the backdoor to allow the wind to whip in earthy smells of cut grass and lilacs.

"Why can't we just talk about it?" Dick implored.

He didn't understand that I could not wrap my mind around snuffing out a life only weeks from the first anniversary of Robert's death.

Employed at *Congressional Quarterly* for only six months when the bold positive on the pregnancy test reset everything, I forced myself to stay focused and steady. Just getting up the courage to inform the managing editor of my unexpected life change required several rehearsals with supportive female colleagues who advised me to look Neil straight in the eye and give him the facts.

"I'm having a baby in late December." Clammy hands gripped shaking knees.

Neil, if stunned, pretended otherwise. "I guess the first thing to say is congratulations."

"Don't worry. I'll only take four weeks maternity leave. And I'll start working weekends to have my write-ups done for the Almanac by the end of the year. Oh, and I have full-time childcare already arranged."

"Take a deep breath," he suggested. "I'm not worried. I know you can do this." His confidence in me solidified my own.

Getting through every day, proving myself at a challenging new job, staying upbeat took the kind of grit that had not come as naturally to me prior to impending maternity.

Dick could not back me off my stubborn stance. "I'm not telling you that you *shouldn't* have this baby," he said. "I just want to have a conversation about possible alternatives."

"I'm not asking you for anything," I screamed. "I'll support this child myself."

"Susan, you're not hearing me."

He was right. I shut him down. He had little choice but to move out, at least until we could figure things out. We went through couples counseling, picked out baby supplies together, often had dinner and watched movies. At a certain point, I had to accept that Dick could not make the commitment. The couples counselor who had been seeing us individually and together for months gently told Dick that he either move back into the Georgetown house or accept that we would be parenting separately. He opted for the latter.

With the baby growing inside me, I could feel tiny movements, hear the softly beating heart, and prepare to become a mother. What I could not do was recognize and grieve another loss. I loved Dick, and part of me will always love him. Deep down, I also knew he would be a better part-time dad and friend than an integral part of a family. What we have instead is mutual respect and the ability to have raised Reid into a terrific young man. We even share considerable moments when we can look back and laugh at all we've been through.

Unexpected things happened. Mary Poppins showed up right on schedule when Reid was one month old. She flew in from grimy England via an American Au Pair program. Though she went by the name Jo and far preferred dancing to MTV with a swaddled Reid than flying about with Dick Van Dyke, this twenty-one-year-old girl performed miracle after miracle in the twelve months she lived with us in Georgetown.

Jo is a beauty (still is, I know, as we stay in touch), with her long auburn hair often streaked in green or purple and a wide impish grin. She took over the household, did the grocery shopping for "bits and bobs" after clipping coupons and tucking Reid into his harness. When I needed a mood uplift, she bought a box of hair color and turned me into a redhead. Facing a difficult deadline on a cover story, and moaning about it, she sent me out for a long run.

"Good thing you two didn't get married," she uttered one day after watching us attempt the assembly of a new stroller. Dick had brought over the tools; I laid the instruction pages on the carpet. The multiple parts would not connect, however, until Jo did her magic. She dismissed us both as useless.

Sadly, her year came to an end. She said goodbye and flew off. Her replacement lasted less than one week.

"We're screwed," I told Dick.

Bill Clinton's inauguration festivities were already in full swing. I, furiously reporting on the new president's policy priorities; Dick, on wire-service duty to cover the galas. We somehow, despite Jo's pathetic assessment of us, managed to juggle. Dick kept Reid during the day; after work, I'd pick Reid up in time for Dick to throw on a suit and attend the night events. I would stroll my little toddler back up Q Street to Dick's apartment in the morning, before plunging into a story on what became the first legislative vehicle President Clinton signed—The Family Leave Act. Before I required coverage under the new law, the Au Pair agency came through with another young woman, very good and qualified. But not Jo.

The other unexpected thing was how enormous a role my mother assumed in raising Reid. Since the Au Pair agency placed strict limits on hours worked, I would keep track of their overtime created by my ten-hour workdays and provide the girls with long stretches of time off to even out the hours. My mother took the train down from Baltimore to care for Reid during those stretches, allowing me to keep working.

Annette Patz, widow, proved a vastly different caretaker than had Annette Kellam, divorcee.

When a tired Reid sucked in air and screamed with full lungs at high treble, this would somehow not rattle her. I would hear my baby halfway down the block and rush in. "Everyone alive?" I'd yell, running the steps to the third-floor nursery.

"The problem is that I can't dance," my mother calmly expounded as I pulled Reid to my breast and let him suck. My lips soothing Reid's downy head, I gave my mother a curious look.

"You know, like what Jo does in front of the television."

"You want to watch MTV?"

"If it makes the baby happy."

Swinging her hips back and forth to rock-and-roll beats replaced her afternoon exercise walks. And Reid swayed with her movement, lulled into blissful sleep tucked in his grandmother's sturdy arms.

Where was this caring woman when Robert and I were growing up?

Early on, she was masquerading as an affluent fifties matron. She often repeated the story of leaving the house in Sudbrook Park with Dad. Robert would lean out the window, screaming for all the neighbors to hear, "How many are you leaving with us tonight?" It generally took two: one nanny to watch me and another to ensure that Robert didn't kill me. I was the disruptive creature who diverted far too much attention from him. Even though my mother wasn't working, she seldom bestowed much maternal affection toward two kids who, seeking her attention, would use a kitchen knife to scratch deep lines into her brand-new dining room table (Robert) and bellow at all hours (me).

After being blindsided by her husband's criminal activity, an essential chunk of my mother shriveled inward, out of reach of two needy children. Emotional distance is my earliest memory of a mother.

Robert would have been more cognizant of the different phases. He enjoyed three undisturbed years of affection from both parents during a time of upward mobility. My arrival marked his first harsh encounter with reality. Mom's already limited attention was suddenly shared with a tiny intruder. When he would jolt me from the crib and drop me to the floor, he learned about discipline. But nothing could prepare him for the day that Dad left.

The distraught mother who took us to live with Grandma Rose did slowly manage to cope with the abysmal twist of fate. She shed years of being her father's favorite Nette, of being a comfortable wartime student at Goucher, and of being the wife of a promising attorney. What emerged was a woman who could accept her circumstances by taking practical steps, like going back to the city's Department of Public Welfare to reapply as a case worker and, without money for nannies, she learned, tentatively, to care for us.

She was so very fragile.

One day, as I sat with her on the green sofa in the den, a sofa where she slept at night, I had badgered her to allow me to cross Stevenson Road and walk up the hill to my cousins' house.

"No," she firmly stated. "You're not old enough." I may have been turning six or seven.

"Robert can go."

"Your brother is older. He knows how to look both ways before crossing a busy road."

"I can do that."

Silence.

"I know how to do that!" I repeated, becoming shrill.

Unable to get a response, I yanked the slipcover from the sofa arm and threw it angrily over her face. Noticing a trembling of her upper body, I inched closer to her and removed the cloth. She was sobbing.

That memory, which frightened me as a little girl, still chills me. I don't recall whether I had the wherewithal to comfort her. Yet, coming to grips with her own vulnerability did gradually give her more capacity to parent.

Over the years, she created a home, both on Stevenson Road and in the small apartment that ensured our basic needs were met. Her life was unquestionably difficult. As a young child, Robert was plagued by stomach ailments. I would often wake up in Grandma Rose's house to sounds of my brother retching. Nearly sleepwalking the length of the long house to the den, I would wake up Mom, who would tuck an infirm and very pale Robert back into bed and clean up the soiled bathroom. My memory holds many recollections of such nights. It is possible that I have magnified the image, that ever-so-slight indication that, before he became the impenetrable Big K, my brother did show signs of inner turmoil.

Robert outgrew his sickliness about the same time he discovered outdoor play with a gang of boys. Many friendships were forged in that subdivision off Stevenson Road, during after-school and weekend baseball and football games on the empty lot in the crossway of family homes. In the years before supervised youth sports, those boys rammed thousands of home runs and touchdowns with no referees or overwrought parents. That's where Robert built strength and learned the power of excelling.

As Robert took his winning stride into the classroom and onto a wider social sphere, my mother finally had someone to lean on. She depended on Robert in so many ways, his excellence casting a glow on her, his personality a font of warmth, his friends a welcome energy in our home.

She slowly developed the sturdiness—many years after the public humiliation of her husband's crimes and the lasting stigma of being divorced—to carry out the tough responsibilities of single parenting.

◆ ◆ ◆

Being a single mom over three decades later proved a very different experience for me. Challenging and exhilarating, I was a real-life Murphy Brown. My family rallied behind me, and Reid raked in loving attention from all sides. Robert's golden stardust had been sprinkled on my son. I would drive him, with his cousins Justin and Jenna, to Harrisburg at Christmas where Dad and Shirley would bestow gifts and memorable happy times. A favorite: Reid sledding down rolling hills tucked within his cousins' arms.

The year Shirley was diagnosed with lung cancer my father declared there would be no Christmas. We went anyway. Those last months of her life sped past far too quickly. I wouldn't give up chances to be with her in the time remaining. Of all the unforgettable moments with my stepmother, one envelops me like cozy fleece on dismal days. With a few softly spoken words, she alone could penetrate the stiff composure that kept me standing the day of Robert's funeral. She had whispered, "You have to always remember how much your brother loved you. He loved you so much."

When my father died three years after Shirley, largely of a broken heart, he left me a precious gift. What I inherited from his estate gave me time, and delicious freedom, to devote to Reid. What he had taken from my mother, my dad returned in kind to me. Limiting my work to freelance articles and being an adjunct professor during Reid's elementary-school years, I could arrange my schedule to be there waiting with the other moms when the children walked out of the classroom.

"What's an adventure?" Reid asked, after I suggested one leaving the school.

"You'll see."

My exhausted first-grader fell asleep as I drove us two hours into the Shenandoah Valley of Virginia, haphazardly following scribbled directions to a dog breeder's house. After a wrong turn up a steep road, I braked at a dead end on a high overlook. While rechecking directions, Reid woke and only saw the green vista of rolling hills far beneath us.

"Is this an adventure?"

"Just the beginning."

That was the day we brought home a companion for Ouija, a little yellow Labrador pup we called Shenandoah. Two dogs and a child inevitably forced a move to the Maryland suburbs. Much as I had once silently denounced my brother for his purchase on a street of homes built to a similar design, I did exactly the same.

◆　◆　◆

Two decades after the Madison Square Garden events, Bonnie Raitt and Jackson Browne performed two antinuclear benefit concerts in Washington, DC and I went—as a journalist. Two segments of my life crashed together, rock politics and single motherhood. After my magazine piece came out depicting the then and now of No Nukes, I explored the more personal angle in a *Washington Post* column that began:

My 6-year-old son, Reid, ran a few smudgy fingers across a 1979 photograph of me grinning broadly from beneath an Annie Hall hat with a No Nukes button flopping on the brim. "You look really dumb, Mom," he blurted.

Friends put it differently: "Boy do you look stoned."

What can I say. When I was asked to recapture the times and aura of the 1970s anti-nuclear movement for a magazine article, I couldn't cut myself out of the picture. I was there amid the protests and all the sex, drugs, and rock-and-roll, and I did inhale.

Seeing Bonnie and Jackson again brought everything back, all the struggle, the commitment, and the being part of a movement. They were helping to publicize a campaign to block creation of a nuclear waste storage facility at Yucca Mountain, deep in the Nevada desert. "It's an insane idea," Bonnie declared at a press conference on the Capitol Steps. "If people were involved, if people knew, they would be outraged. Consider me the town crier."

As a nine-time Grammy winner, Bonnie exhibited none of the tentativeness she had many years earlier speaking on Karen Silkwood. She was bold and dynamic, a real star. Yet the grassroots fervor that once drew thousands of protestors to the Mall had all but dissipated. Hardly anyone was there. I, however, felt a rush when I heard Bonnie denounce the nuclear waste facility.

"Look who's here," she called to Tom Campbell, who wore his graying hair partially Indian-braided. They both embraced me, and I felt that twinge of nostalgia. For a moment, I wanted to join them in speaking to members of Congress. I had to remind myself that I'd become a journalist and could no longer advocate. Besides, I had a six-year old I had to get to soccer practice.

I had also reunited with Howard Kohn and David Fenton in Washington. Their moves to the capital city had preceded my own and, not long after I arrived in 1984, I met the two of them for lunch at a Chinese restaurant in Dupont Circle. Then a stringer for the *Washington Post*, I was attired appropriately in blouse, skirt, and pantyhose. David wore a suit and even Howard had upped his attire to include a tie that matched his jacket. But we were still very much the same people.

"Fenton Communications, really David? How like you to name your public interest firm after yourself," I joked. He'd successfully opened the Washington and New York offices of his firm several years earlier.

We all laughed. The friendship we'd forged a decade earlier had somehow withstood the fallout from the MUSE experience.

Howard said he'd been reading my articles in the *Post*'s Business and Metro sections. "You sound like a professional."

"I am a professional." More laughter.

I saw Howard and David sporadically over the following years on election night gatherings and dinners. I even hired David as a consultant when I ran the communications shop at the then-American Public Welfare Association (now the Public Human Services Association).

Howard's book, *Who Killed Karen Silkwood?* had come out in 1981. He'd sent me a copy inscribed on the cover page with "Thanks for all the help, encouragement, support, and good will over the years. We have come through a lot, and—can you believe it?—it seems worth it, doesn't it?"

Yes, certainly, it was all very much worth it.

CHAPTER 36

Quiet roads still circle around squares of ramblers and split-level homes in the Baltimore subdivision where Grandpa Abe built a house that became my childhood home. The empty lot appropriated by Robert and the other neighborhood boys for throwing around the football is long since buried under concrete and brick. That popular gathering field was not the only undeveloped parcel there. Another, more remote, acre strewn with brambles, fledgling growth, and fallen limbs offered two pre-adolescent girls an escape. Allison and I, paired off by confused emotions neither could articulate, were lucky to find each other. And together, we found solace among branches as broken as us and unruly vines shielding us from the world in a place we dubbed, simply, our *wilderness.*

We lived several blocks apart. How fast, though, our furious peddling brought us together in this wilderness. The bicycles, our imaginary steeds with regal names long forgotten, braced against trees. We had our own codes, our own language, our own titles for things. Even a well-bored tree where we hid notes, only for each other.

As children do, we sometimes fought. I would forget about a prearranged meeting, a serious offense in our wild kingdom. We might bicker over something that happened on the school playground. Or, Allison might order me to peddle my steed home, for crossing her invisible personal barrier.

I had asked to borrow a Rosemary Clooney recording of Irving Berlin's "Sisters, Sisters."

"No, you can't."

I shoved my fist into a pile of gathered pinecones. "I lent you 'Tenderly.'" What mad crushes we both had on Pat Boone.

"I gave it back."

"I'll return 'Sisters, Sisters.'"

Allison's face puffed; she looked away.

"Really, I will."

I should have stopped my pleading long before she asked me to leave.

Allison had lost an older sister to brain cancer. Her parents, like mine, were woefully unprepared to soothe the pain of their two remaining daughters. Allison, the youngest, bore the brunt. During her first five years, the slowly dying sister had consumed every spare moment of her parents' time.

When there were three, the sisters would sometimes dance to Clooney's recording. Of course, I had no way of knowing that.

"I did what I had to do to survive that squelching grief-filled, dysfunctional environment, and good or bad, who that person is has continued to be me inclusive of my life-coping skills," Allison wrote to me in 2018. All we felt there in the *wilderness*, but could never articulate, comes pouring out now every time we communicate.

She had written me a long note when Robert died. By the time I could get back to her, to where she lives in Austin, Texas, I had little left to say.

Then Allison called one day not long after 9/11 and we talked for hours. What struck us was the similitude of our career focus: she a Texas judge in a child protection court; me, writing on child welfare issues. We had both gravitated toward protecting vulnerable children. No coincidence.

Thriving in the long term for Allison, she says, has been validating. She's basically happy in her life, living with the man, also a lawyer, who fathered her two sons. She went through plenty of rough years, nearly flunking out of high school, before grasping the reins of her remarkable intelligence in college.

"Sometimes, like when I'm at the dentist and am completely stressed," she wrote, "they tell me to go to my 'happy place.' It's often the *wilderness*."

◆　◆　◆

Survival is a more multidimensional matter for me. I have grappled for many years with the sad irony that the most-likely-to-succeed Robert succumbed to our childhood blows while I, most likely to do foolish things, have lived to receive a Medicare card and Social Security.

Some days, I envy my brother. Days when being alive is just too much. I become overwhelmed by the unending pattern of small chores imprinting my existence. J. Alfred Prufrock measured out his life with coffee spoons. I weigh the bulk of teabags for the compost pile, think where time has gone. When will it end? Exhaustion grabs me by the throat, but it will never strangle me. Too much in life requires me to be here. I am basically buoyant. Before I could swim, I would jump in to the deep end of the pool and paddle with all my might. Somehow, even now—especially now—I stay afloat.

Unresolved questions about Robert's suicide initiated this chronicled time-warp journey. Going back years and inching forward. Circling and returning to unresolved points. Dissecting what I could not fathom at the time. Throughout this process, I have slowly reconciled my life with the death of a brother who remains burrowed inside me.

Like Allison, through difficult career and child-raising years, I did what I had to do to survive. Our childhoods made us tough.

I have returned to the *wilderness* or, as Allison says, *my happy place*: Seven-and-a-half rural acres in coastal Maine, a salt-water farm of sorts, as my blueberry fields roll down to the clam flats of Sampson Cove and I can see the deep waters of Muscongus Bay from my bedroom window. Allison knew what I had the moment she came to visit me here. Taking in the vast vista, my field of dreams surrounded by thick woods of pine, oak, and birch, she simply smiled.

Moving here, as with my every life twist, was never actually planned. It just happened. Call it feng shui, as my real estate agent did. Something put into play by the baseball coach at Bates College in Lewiston, Maine recruiting Reid for the team. The call came as my former New York City apartment mate, Jayne Loader, was beckoning me to visit the house in Friendship, Maine she had bought with her husband Robert, then a Harvard astrophysicist—a historic waterfront inn, now a very large home, their retreat from Cambridge.

"I'm not going to a college that is smaller than my high school," Reid argued when I informed him of Bates's interest.

I bought the plane tickets. "You only have to visit."

Stressed from work, I could not imagine a better getaway than Maine, especially seeing Jayne, one of my lasting ties to far wilder times. The staid think tank, Brookings Institution, had recruited me four years earlier to be their senior communications expert on domestic policy. Brookings's work substance proved enthralling. The workplace, however, was abysmal. Worn out, I needed a break.

Maine is six hundred miles from Washington—for me, a different galaxy. Something mystic happened during my visit as I watched the late-September sunlight sparking colors from waves crashing against towering rock formations at the Pemaquid Point lighthouse. With the real estate market hitting bottom in 2009, I could not help but notice all the for-sale signs.

When I picked Reid up from his visit at Bates, he told me bluntly that he would not be going to school in Maine.

"That's all right," I told him. "I'm moving to Maine."

Jayne had coaxed me decades earlier from the Upper East Side to Chelsea. Grabbing me out of Washington proved far easier. It just took longer, as I had to get my son off to college.

Reid chose Penn State. I said a silent prayer. My mother did too. Although a good state school, it conjures up a very bad moment in my brother's life—his flunking out, a danger sign that should have been heeded but was not.

Although I like to believe Reid has much of the good about Robert in his DNA, my son is his own person. "Robert was never that happy," my mother often told me. Reid has the ebullient spirit of a Millennial, every option for fun encrypted in his handheld phone.

Having given up baseball, Reid went off to college unencumbered by daily practices or a coach's oversight. Dick and I settled him into the dorms. As we drove off, I watched Reid's swift pivot. He barely waved goodbye. Sure, he got in trouble. Plenty. Reid also graduated in four years with a double major, good job prospects, and as an enduring, nearly obsessive, Nittany Lions football fan.

CHAPTER 37

Robert was thirty-nine when he tied the knot that ended his life and broke my heart. This is a grief that doesn't ease with time. There are too many unanswered questions. "What could I have done to stop him," I ask nearly every day. Only slowly am I realizing the limits of what I could have done. Even so, in the good moments, the very best of times, always there is the nagging question: why isn't he here to share this?

I have experienced the bittersweet of watching both of Robert's children grow up, fall in love, get married, pursue strong careers, and have their own children. Not long before my mother died in 2016 at age ninety-two, we gathered at the home where my brother's remarried widow, Charlene, now lives. Sitting around the swimming pool, the rollicking and laughter spun through an entire afternoon.

Reid threw balls with his cousin Justin into a water hoop. Justin's wife, Laura, sat watching their daughter, an adorable toddler with Robert's face.

"Damn," Reid yelled when he missed the hoop.

"Watch your mouth," Justin chided.

My mother, sitting in the shade, yelled out, "Why are you kids still in that pool? In this heat?"

Everyone laughed.

"Nana," Jenna said. "Being in cool water is a great way to not be too warm."

Justin added, "Nana, if it's cold, you get mad when I don't wear a jacket. Now it's hot. And you're upset that we're trying to stay cool. I think you have a temperature regulation issue. You should get that checked out."

Even my mother laughed. Then, in the graveled voice of a smoker, she blurted, "I wish Robert could be here to see this."

Jenna shot back, "He could have been here, if he'd wanted." My niece's anger was loud and clear.

No, he couldn't, I did not say, but have carefully considered.

I recalled the rabbi's words, how he compared Robert to the brightest center candle of a menorah that could reflect everyone's love, burning that much higher. I have always interpreted that to mean Robert somehow couldn't absorb the multilavished love, merely reflect it, or perhaps deflect it.

But how could I explain to Jenna her father's inability to be saved by love? For all that my brother reflected enormous quantities of love and gave it so selflessly to others, our returned love could never penetrate the armor of his deeply hidden pain. We saw the smiles, heard the laughter, enjoyed the generous spirit. But we could never crack his brilliant disguise.

❖ ❖ ❖

My mother died very slowly, in increments so small, fading away is a more apt description of losing her. She had been furious when I first told her I was moving to Maine. "Can't you wait until I die?" That would have been a very long time, and I needed distance from her.

A therapist had warned me years prior that my unresolved, but unnaturally close, relationship with my mother would make her death, when it came, nearly unbearable for me. As the remaining child, I became her backstop, her emotional vessel, her constant.

There was so much to unravel before I lost her. Every six weeks or so, I took Southwest Airlines from Portland to Baltimore, rented a car, and saw her. I tried to get her to talk about Robert, but she only spoke of him in wistful ways. Admitting, some days, that she knew how badly Robert suffered as a child. She just didn't know what to do.

Uncle Morty's death opened a spigot. I flew in for the funeral and stayed an extra day or two. Over lunch, my mother finally confessed to me that she accepted some responsibility for her son's death. "I know," she said in a shaky raspy voice, "that I should have done things differently. I know I am partly to blame."

Only in coming home to Maine could I process her words. Walking the shoreline at low tide with the dogs. Walled away in my study to write. Being with my cadre of friends over beers at the Narrows Tavern. Here, I could heal.

Annette Patz would not go gently into the dying light. A life-long smoker, she refused to quit, even after chronic obstructive pulmonary disease required occasional tethering to an oxygen tank. Her brittle bones and unsteady gait meant falls and breaks. I would get repeated calls from Charlene or Justin. "She's back in the ER."

When the doctor sent her to rehabilitation for an intended stay of two weeks, she took a look around, sniffed the food, and signed herself out. She had an occasional caregiver, and simply asked the woman to drive her home.

So riled, I ran outside without a coat on a cold, starry night. "Goddammit, Robert!" I yelled. "Why have you left me alone to handle this crazy woman!" As I vocalized loudly into the Maine night air, I could sense my brother. See him shrug. "She's not going to change," he always told me.

My mother seemed to be lingering, the pain softened by morphine and by hospice workers who cared for her in the final months. "There's something that she hasn't resolved," the hospice nurse told me. "She can't die until that is done."

I tried to get her to open up about Robert, but she acted as if she couldn't hear me. One day I screamed, "Don't you ever think about Robert?"

My mother turned slowly to look at me. "Every day and in every way," she whispered in what voice she had left.

They say that people close to death can see and converse with their loved ones who have already passed. She admitted to talking with her mother. But I believe she waited for Robert and wouldn't go until he came and took her himself. Perhaps he carried her across, as she had been wheelchair bound for many months. She could barely breathe without oxygen when she died late one night. I wasn't there, but I know how she finally left this world, in the only way she would, once again embracing the most precious thing from her life.

With her final departure, I could begin this journey.

ACKNOWLEDGMENTS

It's taken me nearly a lifetime of experiences to fill this book and a good decade to put that chaos into words. I've had so many people cheering me on, and one person who significantly redirected my journey: Julie Stevenson with Massie & McQuilkin Literary Agency. She enjoyed the behind-the-scenes look at *Rolling Stone* and MUSE but strongly suggested that I bring my relationship with my brother to the forefront and minimize the nitty gritty of concert planning. Although she did not represent me, her advice shuffled me in a different, and far more difficult, direction. I had to understand why my brother Robert took his life. Through the patient guidance of Laura Zegel during five years of therapy, I did ultimately come to grips with what happened.

Brilliant Disguise is substantially different from *Was Only Rock & Roll*, the book I initially wrote.

I'm not sure that I could have taken this journey anywhere but in Waldoboro, Maine. Without this coastline, the Narrows Tavern, and an amazing cast of characters, I may not have remained buoyant long enough to carry this through to the end. To Laura, Brian, Susan, Morganne, Marcia, Mary, Melissa, Erin, Mark, Jann, Mauri, Eric, Josh, Allan, Travis, and so many more, the next beer is on me.

Finally, my nephew Justin proved a wonderful and patient sounding board throughout this process; my niece Jenna told me from the start that it was my story and to say it any way I like; and my son, Reid, well, maybe one day he will actually read this memoir.

Milton Keynes UK
Ingram Content Group UK Ltd.
UKHW010702220524
443011UK00003B/45